Betty Crocker's

CASUAL COUNTRY COOKING

PRENTICE HALL

NEW YORK   LONDON   TORONTO   SYDNEY   TOKYO   SINGAPORE

PRENTICE HALL GENERAL REFERENCE
15 Columbus Circle
New York, New York, 10023

Library of Congress Cataloging-in-Publication data

Crocker, Betty.
   [Casual country cooking]
   Betty Crocker's casual country cooking.
      p.   cm.
   Includes index.
   ISBN 0-671-79923-1
   1. Cookery, American.   I. Title.
TX715.C92139   1993
641.5973—dc20   92-32344
                                                 CIP

Designed by Levavi & Levavi

Manufactured in the United States of America

10 9 8 7 6 5 4 3 2 1

First Edition

CREDITS

GENERAL MILLS, INC.

Betty Crocker Food and Publications Center
   Director, Marcia Copeland
   Editor, Lois Tlusty
   Recipe Development, Mary Hallin Johnson
   Food Stylists, Mary Sethre, Kate Courtney Condon
Nutrition Department
   Nutritionist, Nancy Holmes, R.D.
Photographic Services
   Photographer, Nanoi Doonan Dixon

Contents

Casual Country Menus

Southwest Ranch Supper

Fresh Tomato Salsa with Tortilla Chips*
Chicken-fried Steak
Hashed Brown Potatoes*
Avocado Citrus Salad
Chili-Cheese Corn Bread
Creamy Rice Pudding or
Blackberry Jam Cake
Sangria* — Iced Tea*

Old-fashioned Barbecue

Barbecued Spareribs
Fried Chicken
Coleslaw
Country Potato Salad
Traditional Corn Bread
Citrus-Peach Shortcake
Lemonade*

Oregon Trail Feast

Broiled Salmon with Hazelnut Butter
Steamed New Potatoes*
Pacific Green Beans
Sourdough Bread*
Blackberry Cobbler and Honey Walnut Pie

*Recipes for these menu items are not included in
this book.

Midwest Potluck

Minnesota Wild Rice Soup
Meat Loaf
Ham and Scalloped Potatoes
Skillet Acorn Squash
Peas and Cheese Salad
Heartland Three-Bean Salad
Corn Relish and Bread and Butter Pickles
Rhubarb Crisp and Deep-Dish Apple Pie

New England Church Supper

New Hampshire Cheese Soup
New England Boiled Dinner
Baked Beans*
Old-fashioned Coleslaw
Blueberry Muffins
Maple-Apple Pie and Snickerdoodles

Southern Thanksgiving Dinner

Turkey with Corn Bread Stuffing
Glazed Baked Ham
Mashed Potatoes*
Cheesy Grits
Candied Sweet Potatoes
Perfection Salad
Watermelon Pickles
Dixie Biscuits
Sweet Potato Pie and Pound Cake*

Introduction

We all have our favorite country food memories: yeast dough rising on the counter, then spreading the aroma of freshly baked bread through the house; scrubbed new potatoes from the garden, ready for a hearty stew; and abundant, fragrant herbs. Whether it's for family or friends, the down-home recipes found here will bring to mind the abundance of orchards and fields, even if you work in an office all day!

Our rich country culinary heritage is based on contributions of Native Americans and settlers alike. They made delicious and creative use of local ingredients—corn for puddings and breads, clams for chowder, berries and fruits for pies and cobblers, catfish for easy dinners, roasted turkey with stuffings flavored with local ingredients, such as chestnuts. To this native bounty, settlers added recipes from the "old world," creating a harmonious table and bringing us such favorites as coleslaw, potato salad and even apple pie.

Country cooking was a necessity when the majority of the population lived on farms and there were few labor-saving devices. Today, we have access to many kitchen appliances that save time and labor and most of us have busy lives in or near cities. Our recipes keep all of the flavor and charm of the country but are tailored for modern homes and busy lifestyles. The Mixed Berry Jam, also known as "freezer jam," lets you make homemade jam in less than half an hour by relying on the freezer for preservation. And, the Baked Apple Butter lets you pop the mixture in the oven, then go about your business, without constant stirring and watching.

Satisfy your taste for good country cooking with the freshness and wholesome appeal of *Betty Crocker's Casual Country Cooking*. We're sure you'll agree, whether you have been plowing the South forty or running a carpool, come mealtime, these recipes are sure to please!

THE BETTY CROCKER EDITORS

1

Farm-fresh Poultry and Fish

Poultry and fish were mainstays of the early settlers. Just about every farmer raised chickens, while turkey and fish were plentiful in the woods and streams. Each region created its own unique recipes for these staples, such as southern Brunswick Stew, Maryland Crab Cakes and New England Clam Chowder.

We've also included universal favorites, well-loved dishes wherever they are served—spicy Baked Barbecued Chicken, comforting Chicken Pot Pie, and fresh Broiled Trout. And while everyone agrees that tender roast turkey is a classic, no one seems to agree on what is the very best stuffing for this noble bird. That's why we've served up a regional collection of the best stuffing recipes in the country, from chestnut stuffing to corn bread stuffing.

Fried Chicken (page 2)

Baked Barbecued Chicken

¹/₄ cup (¹/₂ stick) margarine or butter

2¹/₂- to 3-pound cut-up broiler-fryer chicken

1 cup ketchup

¹/₂ cup water

¹/₄ cup lemon juice

1 tablespoon Worcestershire sauce

2 teaspoons paprika

¹/₂ teaspoon salt

1 medium onion, finely chopped (about ¹/₂ cup)

1 clove garlic, finely chopped

Heat oven to 375°. Heat margarine in rectangular pan, 13 × 9 × 2 inches, in oven. Place chicken in margarine, turning to coat. Arrange skin side down in pan. Bake uncovered 30 minutes.

Mix remaining ingredients in 1-quart saucepan. Heat to boiling; remove from heat. Drain fat from chicken; turn skin side up. Spoon sauce over chicken. Bake uncovered until thickest pieces are done and juices of chicken run clear, about 30 minutes longer. *6 servings.*

GRILLED BARBECUED CHICKEN: Cover and grill chicken, bone sides down, 4 to 5 inches from medium coals, 25 minutes. Prepare sauce as directed. Turn chicken. Grill until thickest pieces are done, turning and brushing frequently with sauce, 30 to 40 minutes.

Nutrition Information Per Serving

1 serving

Calories	350	Fat, g	20
Protein, g	28	Cholesterol, mg	85
Carbohydrate, g	14	Sodium, mg	840

Fried Chicken

Fried chicken used to be the Sunday dinner of choice in the summer, the time when the spring chickens in the barnyard reached the right size for frying. Most cooks swear by a heavy cast-iron skillet for frying chicken, to make it crisp on the outside, moist and tender on the inside.

¹/₂ cup all-purpose flour

1 teaspoon salt

1 teaspoon paprika

¹/₄ teaspoon pepper

2¹/₂- to 3-pound cut-up broiler-fryer chicken

Vegetable oil

Creamy Gravy (right)

Mix flour, salt, paprika and pepper. Coat chicken with flour mixture. Heat oil (¹/₄ inch) in 12-inch skillet over medium-high heat until hot. Cook chicken in oil until light brown on all sides, about 10 minutes; reduce heat. Cover tightly and simmer, turning once or twice, until thickest pieces are done and juices of chicken run clear, about 35 minutes. If skillet cannot be covered tightly, add 1 to 2 tablespoons water. Remove cover during last 5 minutes of cooking to crisp chicken. Remove chicken; keep warm. Prepare Creamy Gravy; serve with chicken. *6 servings.*

CREAMY GRAVY

2 tablespoons all-purpose flour
1/2 cup chicken broth or water
1/2 cup milk
Salt and pepper to taste

Pour drippings from skillet into bowl, leaving brown particles in skillet. Return 2 tablespoons drippings to skillet. Stir in flour. Cook over low heat, stirring constantly, until smooth and bubbly; remove from heat. Stir in broth and milk. Heat to boiling, stirring constantly. Boil and stir 1 minute. Stir in a few drops browning sauce, if desired. Stir in salt and pepper.

BUTTERMILK-FRIED CHICKEN: Increase flour to 1 cup, salt to 1½ teaspoons and paprika to 2 teaspoons. Dip chicken into 1 cup buttermilk before coating with flour mixture.

Nutrition Information Per Serving

1 serving

Calories	400	Fat, g	28
Protein, g	25	Cholesterol, mg	70
Carbohydrate, g	11	Sodium, mg	670

Chicken Pot Pie

Traditionally, whenever fried chicken was made (whether for Sunday dinner, a picnic or a potluck supper), cooks saved the pan drippings in the icebox. The next day, the drippings were made into gravy and combined with leftover chicken and vegetables for chicken pot pie. Many cooks liked to personalize their pot pies, some preferring a lattice top and others using small cookie cutters to cut openings for the steam.

1/3 cup margarine or butter
1/3 cup all-purpose flour
1/3 cup chopped onion
1/2 teaspoon salt
1/4 teaspoon pepper
1¾ cups chicken or turkey broth
2/3 cup milk
2½ to 3 cups cut-up cooked chicken or turkey
*1 cup shelled fresh green peas**
*1 cup diced carrots**
Pastry for 9-inch two-crust pie

Heat margarine in 2-quart saucepan over low heat until melted. Stir in flour, onion, salt and pepper. Cook, stirring constantly, until mixture is bubbly; remove from heat. Stir in broth and milk. Heat to boiling, stirring constantly. Boil and stir 1 minute. Stir in chicken, peas and carrots.

Heat oven to 425°. Prepare Pastry. Roll two-thirds of the pastry into 13-inch square; ease into ungreased square pan, 9 × 9 × 2 inches. Pour chicken mixture into pastry-lined pan. Roll remaining pastry into 11-inch square. Fold pastry in half and cut slits near center so steam can escape. Place square over filling; turn edges under and flute. Bake until golden brown, about 35 minutes. *6 servings.*

Nutrition Information Per Serving

1 serving

Calories	575	Fat, g	36
Protein, g	25	Cholesterol, mg	50
Carbohydrate, g	38	Sodium, mg	1000

*1 package (10 ounces) frozen peas and carrots can be substituted for the fresh peas and carrots. Rinse with cold water to separate; drain.

Chicken Fricassee

Chicken Fricassee is another well-loved "Sunday" meal. Although fried chicken is often made with tender spring chickens, traditional fricassee is made with mature hens. The hen is slowly simmered until tender, then topped with fluffy dumplings. Old-fashioned mashed potatoes topped with the well-seasoned gravy from this dish make a perfect accompaniment. In this recipe, we have substituted the faster-cooking broiler-fryer for the traditional stewing hen, for the same great flavor in less time than ever.

1/4 cup (1/2 stick) margarine or butter

3- to 4-pound cut-up broiler-fryer chicken

2 cups water

2 medium carrots, sliced (about 1 cup)

1 medium onion, chopped (about 1/2 cup)

1 teaspoon salt

2 teaspoons chopped fresh or 1/2 teaspoon dried thyme leaves

2 whole cloves

1 bay leaf

3 tablespoons all-purpose flour

1/2 cup milk or water

1/8 teaspoon pepper

Parsley Dumplings (below)

Heat margarine in Dutch oven or 12-inch skillet over medium-high heat until margarine is melted. Cook chicken in margarine until brown on all sides, 15 to 20 minutes. Drain margarine from Dutch oven. Stir in water, carrots, onion, salt, thyme, cloves and bay leaf. Heat to boiling; reduce heat. Cover and simmer until chicken is done, 40 to 50 minutes.

Remove chicken; keep warm. Remove bay leaf. Mix flour, milk and pepper until smooth; pour into Dutch oven. Heat to boiling, stirring constantly. Boil and stir 1 minute; reduce heat. Return chicken to Dutch oven.

Prepare Parsley Dumplings. Drop by rounded tablespoonfuls onto hot chicken (do not drop directly on liquid). Cover tightly; cook until dumplings are fluffy and dry on top, 10 to 14 minutes. *6 servings.*

PARSLEY DUMPLINGS

1 1/4 cups all-purpose flour
2 tablespoons chopped fresh parsley
2 teaspoons baking powder
1/2 teaspoon salt
3 tablespoons margarine or butter
2/3 cup milk

Mix flour, parsley, baking powder and salt in 2-quart bowl. Cut in margarine until mixture resembles fine crumbs. Stir in milk.

Nutrition Information Per Serving

1 serving

Calories	480	Fat, g	26
Protein, g	32	Cholesterol, mg	85
Carbohydrate, g	30	Sodium, mg	920

Brunswick Stew

North Carolina; Georgia; and Brunswick County, Virginia, have all claimed to be the birthplace of this traditional southern stew. A long-time favorite at outdoor gatherings such as picnics and family reunions, Brunswick Stew was originally made with wild game, including squirrel, raccoon and opossum. This updated recipe uses easier-to-find chicken and salt pork for equally delicious results.

3- to 3¹/₂-pound cut-up broiler-fryer chicken

4 cups water

1 teaspoon salt

¹/₄ teaspoon pepper

Dash of ground red pepper (cayenne)

2 cans (16 ounces each) whole tomatoes, undrained

2 cups fresh whole kernel corn*

2 cups fresh lima beans**

1 medium potato, cut into cubes (about 1 cup)

1 medium onion, chopped (about ¹/₂ cup)

¹/₄ pound lean salt pork or bacon, cut into 1-inch pieces

¹/₂ cup water

2 tablespoons all-purpose flour

Remove any excess fat from chicken. Heat chicken, giblets, neck, 4 cups water and the salt to boiling in Dutch oven; reduce heat. Cover and simmer until thickest pieces of chicken are done and juices of chicken run clear, about 1 hour. Skim fat from broth. Remove skin and bones from chicken if desired; return chicken to broth. Stir in pepper, red pepper, tomatoes, corn, beans, potato, onion and salt pork. Heat to boiling; reduce heat. Simmer uncovered 1 hour. Shake ¹/₂ cup water and the flour in tightly covered container. Stir into stew. Heat to boiling, stirring constantly. Boil and stir 1 minute. *8 servings.*

Nutrition Information Per Serving

1 serving

Calories	310	Fat, g	12
Protein, g	24	Cholesterol, mg	55
Carbohydrate, g	27	Sodium, mg	860

*1 package (10 ounces) frozen whole kernel corn or 1 can (17 ounces) whole kernel corn, undrained, can be substituted for the fresh corn.

**1 package (10 ounces) frozen lima beans or 1 can (16 ounces) lima beans, undrained, can be substituted for the fresh lima beans.

Country Captain

½ cup all-purpose flour

1 teaspoon salt

¼ teaspoon pepper

2½- to 3-pound cut-up broiler-fryer chicken

¼ cup vegetable oil

1½ teaspoons curry powder

1½ teaspoons chopped fresh or ½ teaspoon dried thyme leaves

¼ teaspoon salt

1 large onion, chopped (about 1 cup)

1 large green bell pepper, chopped (about 1½ cups)

1 clove garlic, finely chopped, or ⅛ teaspoon garlic powder

1 can (16 ounces) whole tomatoes, undrained

¼ cup currants or raisins

⅓ cup slivered almonds, toasted

3 cups hot cooked rice

Heat oven to 350°. Mix flour, 1 teaspoon salt and the pepper. Coat chicken with flour mixture. Heat oil in 10-inch skillet until hot. Cook chicken in oil over medium heat until light brown, 15 to 20 minutes. Place chicken in ungreased 2½-quart casserole. Drain oil from skillet.

Add curry powder, thyme, ¼ teaspoon salt, the onion, bell pepper, garlic and tomatoes to skillet. Heat to boiling, stirring frequently to loosen brown particles from skillet. Pour over chicken. Cover and bake until thickest pieces are done and juices of chicken run clear, about 40 minutes. Skim fat from liquid if necessary; add currants. Bake uncovered 5 minutes. Sprinkle with almonds. Serve with rice and, if desired, grated fresh coconut and chutney. *6 servings.*

Nutrition Information Per Serving

1 serving			
Calories	520	Fat, g	23
Protein, g	29	Cholesterol, mg	70
Carbohydrate, g	49	Sodium, mg	1020

Country Captain

Roast Turkey with Stuffing

Choose one of our delicious stuffings on the following pages, or use a favorite tried-and-true stuffing recipe of your own.

Stuffing (see pages 10–11)
10- to 12-pound turkey
Margarine or butter, melted

Prepare stuffing. Fill wishbone area with stuffing. Fasten neck skin to back with skewer. Fold wings across back with tips touching. Fill body cavity lightly with stuffing. (Do not pack—stuffing will expand.) Tuck drumsticks under band of skin at tail or skewer to tail.

Heat oven to 325°. Place turkey, breast side up, on rack in shallow roasting pan. Brush with margarine. Insert meat thermometer so tip is in thickest part of inside thigh muscle or thickest part of breast meat and does not touch bone. (Tip of thermometer can be inserted in center of stuffing.) Do not add water. Do not cover. Place a tent of aluminum foil loosely over turkey when it begins to turn golden. When two-thirds done, cut band or remove skewer holding legs.

Roast until done and juices of turkey run clear, 3½ to 4½ hours. Turkey is done when thermometer placed in meat registers 185° or in stuffing registers 165° or drumstick meat feels very soft.

Let stand about 20 minutes before carving. As soon as possible after serving, remove all stuffing from turkey. Promptly refrigerate stuffing and turkey separately; use within 2 days. *10 servings.*

Nutrition Information Per Serving

1 serving turkey only

Calories	590	Fat, g	22
Protein, g	98	Cholesterol, mg	280
Carbohydrate, g	0	Sodium, mg	280

Roast Turkey with Rice Stuffing (page 11);
Candied Sweet Potatoes (page 58)

Sensational Stuffings ✢✢✢✢✢✢✢

Stuffing, or dressing, as it is sometimes called, has been a common sight on American tables since colonial days. Usually well seasoned, and based on a mixture of bread crumbs or cubes, it is used to stuff poultry, fish, meat and vegetables. While stuffing may offer the advantage of "stretching" a particular dish, we usually make it just because it tastes so good! The Plimouth Plantation Cookbook *(note the original spelling of Plymouth, Massachusetts) shows us that the Pilgrims fancied spicy, sweet stuffings instead of the savory, often sage-flavored stuffings so popular today.*

Chestnut Stuffing

When we think of a Thanksgiving turkey with all the trimmings, a traditional Victorian-era chestnut stuffing may come to mind. Early settlers used chestnuts that grew in forests from Maine to Alabama. When nearly all the trees were killed in the Great Chestnut Blight of 1904, Americans were forced to turn to southern Europe for a supply of the shiny brown nuts. Look for fresh chestnuts around Thanksgiving, when they usually become available. Their distinctive flavor makes this recipe from the Northeast absolutely delicious.

1 pound chestnuts

3 medium stalks celery (with leaves), chopped (about 1½ cups)

1 large onion, finely chopped (about ¾ cup)

1 cup (2 sticks) margarine or butter

7 cups soft bread cubes

1½ teaspoons salt

2 tablespoon chopped fresh or 1½ teaspoons dried sage leaves

1 tablespoon chopped fresh or 1 teaspoon dried thyme leaves

½ teaspoon pepper

Cut X shape on rounded side of each chestnut. Heat chestnuts and enough water to cover to boiling. Boil uncovered 10 minutes; drain. Remove shells and skins. Heat chestnuts and enough water to cover to boiling. Boil uncovered 10 minutes; drain and chop.

Cook and stir celery, onion and margarine in 10-inch skillet until onion is tender. Stir in about one-third of the bread cubes. Turn mixture into deep bowl. Add remaining bread cubes, the salt, sage, thyme, pepper and chestnuts; toss. *10 servings (½ cup each).*

Nutrition Information Per Serving

1 serving			
Calories	290	Fat, g	20
Protein, g	3	Cholesterol, mg	0
Carbohydrate, g	24	Sodium, mg	660

Corn Bread Stuffing

To take advantage of plentiful ingredients, corn bread stuffing was one of the favorite early stuffings. Our Corn Bread Stuffing is based on recipes of southern African Americans but also shows the influences of Native Americans and white sharecroppers. Simple and basic, it reflects the limited resources available to the cooks of earlier days.

2 medium stalks celery (with leaves), chopped (about 1 cup)

1 large onion, chopped (about 1 cup)

1/2 cup (1 stick) margarine or butter

5 cups crumbled corn bread

3 cups soft bread cubes

1/2 cup chicken broth

2 teaspoons poultry seasoning

1/2 teaspoon salt

1/2 teaspoon ground sage

1/2 teaspoon ground thyme

1/4 teaspoon pepper

Cook and stir celery, onion and margarine in Dutch oven over medium-high heat until celery is tender, about 3 minutes. Stir in corn bread and bread cubes. Cook, stirring occasionally, until bread is golden brown, about 10 minutes; remove from heat. Add remaining ingredients; toss. *16 servings (1/2 cup each).*

Nutrition Information Per Serving

1 serving

Calories	175	Fat, g	10
Protein, g	3	Cholesterol, mg	15
Carbohydrate, g	18	Sodium, mg	350

Rice Stuffing

Rice has been abundant and relatively inexpensive for the last half century, which has made it a popular ingredient in everything from salads and soups to side dishes and stuffings. Our recipe for Rice Stuffing comes from southern Texas, where it is used in crown roasts of pork and pork chops, in addition to poultry. Do not pack tightly, because stuffing needs room to expand during cooking.

1 medium stalk celery (with leaves), chopped (about 1/2 cup)

1 small onion, chopped (about 1/4 cup)

2 tablespoons margarine or butter

1/2 teaspoon salt

1/8 teaspoon pepper

2 cups cooked rice

1/2 cup chopped walnuts

1/3 cup raisins

1/4 teaspoon paprika

4 slices bacon, crisply cooked and crumbled

Cook celery, onion, margarine, salt and pepper in 10-inch skillet until celery is tender; remove from heat. Stir in remaining ingredients. *8 servings (1/2 cup each).*

FRUITED RICE STUFFING: Omit raisins. Stir in 1/3 cup cut-up prunes and 1/3 cup cut-up dried apricots.

Nutrition Information Per Serving

1 serving

Calories	180	Fat, g	9
Protein, g	3	Cholesterol, mg	5
Carbohydrate, g	22	Sodium, mg	420

Baked Chicken and Rice

This hearty favorite is based on a traditional Spanish recipe, *Arroz con Pollo*, "chicken with rice." A specialty of Mexico and Puerto Rico, this classic dish is especially popular in the southwestern United States.

2¹/₂- to 3-pound cut-up broiler-fryer chicken

³/₄ teaspoon salt

¹/₄ to ¹/₂ teaspoon paprika

¹/₄ teaspoon pepper

2¹/₂ cups chicken broth

1 cup uncooked regular long grain rice

1 medium onion, chopped (about ¹/₂ cup)

1 clove garlic, finely chopped

¹/₂ teaspoon salt

1¹/₂ teaspoons chopped fresh or ¹/₂ teaspoon dried oregano leaves

¹/₈ teaspoon ground turmeric

1 bay leaf

2 cups shelled fresh green peas*

Pimiento strips

Pitted ripe olives

Heat oven to 350°. Place chicken, skin sides up, in ungreased rectangular baking dish, 13 × 9 × 2 inches. Sprinkle with salt, paprika and pepper. Bake uncovered 30 minutes.

Heat broth to boiling. Remove chicken and drain fat from dish. Mix broth, rice, onion, garlic, salt, oregano, turmeric, bay leaf and peas in baking dish. Top with chicken. Cover with aluminum foil and bake until rice and thickest pieces of chicken are done and liquid is absorbed, about 30 minutes. Remove bay leaf. Top with pimiento strips and olives. *6 servings.*

Nutrition Information Per Serving

1 serving

Calories	370	Fat, g	12
Protein, g	29	Cholesterol, mg	70
Carbohydrate, g	36	Sodium, mg	920

*1 package (10 ounces) frozen green peas, thawed and drained, can be substituted for the fresh green peas.

Wild Rice–stuffed Northern Pike

Wild Rice Stuffing (below)

2¹/₂- to 3-pound northern pike, cleaned

Lemon juice

Salt

Vegetable oil

¹/₄ cup (¹/₂ stick) margarine or butter, melted

2 tablespoons lemon juice

Lemon wedges

Prepare Wild Rice Stuffing. Heat oven to 350°. Pat pike dry inside and out. Rub cavity of pike with lemon juice; sprinkle with salt. Loosely stuff with Wild Rice Stuffing. Close opening with skewers and lace with string. (Spoon any remaining stuffing into buttered baking dish; cover and refrigerate. Place in oven with pike 30 minutes before pike is done.) Brush pike with oil; place in shallow roasting pan. Mix margarine and 2 tablespoons lemon juice. Bake pike uncovered, brushing occasionally with margarine mixture, until pike flakes easily with fork, 50 to 60 minutes. Serve with lemon wedges. *6 servings*.

WILD RICE STUFFING

³/₄ uncooked wild rice

2 cups water

1¹/₂ teaspoons chicken bouillon granules

1 medium stalk celery (with leaves), thinly sliced (about ¹/₂ cup)

1 medium onion, chopped (about ¹/₂ cup)

¹/₄ cup slivered almonds

¹/₄ cup (¹/₂ stick) margarine or butter

8 ounces mushrooms, sliced (about 3 cups)

Heat rice, water and bouillon granules to boiling, stirring once or twice; reduce heat. Cover and simmer until tender, 40 to 50 minutes. After cooking rice 30 minutes, check to see that rice is not sticking to pan. Add 2 to 3 tablespoons water if necessary.

Cook and stir celery, onion and almonds in margarine in 10-inch skillet over medium heat until vegetables are tender and almonds are light brown. Add mushrooms; cook until tender, about 5 minutes longer. Stir in wild rice.

Nutrition Information Per Serving

1 serving

Calories	435	Fat, g	22
Protein, g	37	Cholesterol, mg	90
Carbohydrate, g	22	Sodium, mg	1000

Southern-fried Catfish

Pan-fried catfish used to be a southern secret, but it seems the rest of the country has caught on. Dipped in seasoned cornmeal and quickly fried, catfish served with hush puppies and coleslaw steals the show at southern fish fries. Found naturally in the Mississippi River and southern inland waterways, catfish are also farmed in several states of the Mississippi Delta.

Vegetable oil

1¹/₄ cup cornmeal

1 teaspoon salt

¹/₂ teaspoon ground red pepper (cayenne)

¹/₄ teaspoon pepper

6 small catfish (about ¹/₂ pound each), skinned and pan dressed

¹/₂ cup all-purpose flour

2 eggs, slightly beaten

Heat oven to 275°. Heat oil (¹/₂ inch) in 12-inch skillet over medium-high heat until hot. Mix cornmeal, salt, red pepper and pepper; reserve.

Coat catfish with flour; dip into eggs. Coat with cornmeal mixture. Fry catfish, 2 at a time, until golden brown, about 6 minutes on each side. Keep warm in oven while frying remaining catfish. Garnish with lemon wedges if desired. *6 servings.*

Nutrition Information Per Serving

1 serving

Calories	525	Fat, g	23
Protein, g	48	Cholesterol, mg	190
Carbohydrate, g	31	Sodium, mg	430

Southern-fried Catfish, Apple-Cheese Coleslaw (page 56), Hush Puppies (page 70)

Broiled Salmon with Hazelnut Butter

Salmon and hazelnuts are both native to—and favorites of—the Pacific Northwest. Fresh king salmon, largest of the Pacific salmon, and silver salmon, with its deep coral color, are especially prized. You'll find the delicate Hazelnut Butter a wonderful topping for fish, vegetables and poultry.

Hazelnut Butter (below)
4 salmon fillets (1 to 1½ pounds)
½ teaspoon salt
⅛ teaspoon pepper

Prepare Hazelnut Butter. Set oven control to broil. Grease shallow roasting pan or jelly roll pan, 15½ × 10½ × 1 inch. Sprinkle both sides of fish with salt and pepper. Place in pan. Broil fish with tops 4 to 6 inches from heat 4 minutes; turn and spread each fillet with about 1 tablespoon Hazelnut Butter. Broil until fish flakes easily with fork, 4 to 8 minutes. *4 servings*.

HAZELNUT BUTTER

2 tablespoons finely chopped hazelnuts
3 tablespoons margarine or butter, softened
1 tablespoon chopped fresh parsley
1 teaspoon lemon juice

Heat oven to 350°. Spread hazelnuts on ungreased cookie sheet. Bake until golden brown, 4 to 6 minutes, stirring occasionally; cool. Mix with remaining ingredients.

Nutrition Information Per Serving

1 serving			
Calories	255	Fat, g	17
Protein, g	25	Cholesterol, mg	45
Carbohydrate, g	1	Sodium, mg	420

Broiled Salmon with Hazelnut Butter

Broiled Trout

4 rainbow trout or other small fish (6 to 8 ounces each), cleaned, boned and butterflied

¹/₄ cup (¹/₂ stick) margarine or butter, melted

2 tablespoons lemon juice

1 tablespoon chopped fresh parsley

Salt

Paprika

Set oven control to broil. Grease broiler pan. Place fish in pan, skin sides down. Mix margarine, lemon juice and parsley; brush on fish. Sprinkle lightly with salt and paprika. Broil fish with tops 4 inches from heat until fish flakes easily with fork, 5 to 6 minutes. *4 servings.*

Nutrition Information Per Serving

1 serving

Calories	300	Fat, g	17
Protein, g	35	Cholesterol, mg	95
Carbohydrate, g	1	Sodium, mg	710

Maryland Crab Cakes

According to locals on Maryland's eastern shore, fresh blue crabs from the Chesapeake Bay provide the best crabmeat in the world! But if you can't get to Maryland, you'll find that any lump crabmeat will make for light and fluffy crab cakes. Carefully pick through the crabmeat to remove bits of shell and cartilage. For an irresistible meal, serve hot crab cakes with fresh lemon slices or top each with a dollop of tangy tartar sauce.

1 pound crabmeat, cooked, cartilage removed, and flaked (2¹/₂ to 3 cups)

1¹/₂ cups soft white bread crumbs (without crusts)

2 tablespoons margarine or butter, melted

1 teaspoon dry mustard

¹/₂ teaspoon salt

¹/₈ teaspoon pepper

2 egg yolks, beaten

Vegetable oil

Mix all ingredients except oil. Shape into 4 patties, each about 3¹/₂ inches in diameter. Refrigerate until firm, about 1¹/₂ hours.

Heat oil (1 inch) to 375°. Fry patties until golden brown on both sides, 4 to 5 minutes; drain. *4 servings.*

Nutrition Information Per Serving

1 serving

Calories	315	Fat, g	24
Protein, g	19	Cholesterol, mg	190
Carbohydrate, g	6	Sodium, mg	630

Seafood Gumbo

Gumbo is a perfect example of why America is "the Great Melting Pot." Back in the eighteenth century, French Canadians who settled in the bayou country southwest of New Orleans became known as Cajuns. They made a hearty soup-stew. Creoles, locals of Spanish and/or French descent, added hot red pepper to the stew. And African Americans contributed okra, a native African vegetable, to thicken it.

1 large onion, chopped (about 1 cup)

1 medium green bell pepper, chopped (about 1 cup)

2 medium stalks celery, chopped (about 1 cup)

1¹/₂ pounds fresh okra, cut into ¹/₂-inch pieces*

2 cloves garlic, crushed

¹/₄ cup (¹/₂ stick) plus 2 tablespoons margarine, butter or lard

¹/₂ cup all-purpose flour

1 can (16 ounces) whole tomatoes, undrained

5 cups chicken broth, clam juice or water

2 teaspoons salt

¹/₂ teaspoon white pepper

¹/₂ teaspoon black pepper

¹/₂ teaspoon ground red pepper (cayenne)

2 bay leaves

1 pound raw medium shrimp, peeled and deveined

³/₄ pound cooked lump crabmeat

3 cups hot cooked rice

Mix onion, bell pepper, celery, okra and garlic; reserve. To make roux, heat margarine in 6- to 8-quart Dutch oven over medium heat until hot. Gradually stir in flour. Cook, stirring constantly, until caramel colored, about 7 minutes.

Add half of reserved onion mixture. Cook, stirring constantly, about 1 minute. Stir in remaining onion mixture. Cook until celery is crisp-tender, about 4 minutes. Stir in and break up tomatoes. Stir in chicken broth, salt, white pepper, black pepper, red pepper and bay leaves. Heat to boiling; reduce heat. Simmer uncovered, stirring occasionally, 1 hour.

Add shrimp and crabmeat to Dutch oven. Heat to boiling. Boil uncovered 1¹/₂ minutes; remove from heat. Cover and let stand 15 minutes. Stir and remove bay leaves. Serve over rice. *8 servings.*

Nutrition Information Per Serving

1 serving			
Calories	345	Fat, g	11
Protein, g	22	Cholesterol, mg	95
Carbohydrate, g	40	Sodium, mg	1690

*2 packages (10 ounces each) frozen cut okra, thawed and drained, can be substituted for the fresh okra.

New England Clam Chowder

New Englanders claim to have invented chowder, and they're famous for serving up a hearty all-white clam chowder. Clam chowder evolved from a traditional fisherman's dish, made up of layers of salt pork, fish and dough (or ship's biscuits) cooked in a kettle in the French tradition. In the early nineteenth century, water was added to the mixture to make it more of a stew. Before long, milk replaced the water, clams were used instead of fish and potatoes took the place of the dough. To finish off this famous chowder, sprinkle with paprika, fresh chives, parsley, tarragon or dill.

1/4 cup cut-up bacon or lean salt pork

1 medium onion, chopped (about 1/2 cup)

2 cans (6 1/2 ounces each) minced clams, drained and liquid reserved

2 medium potatoes, diced (about 2 cups)

Dash of pepper

2 cups milk

Cook and stir bacon and onion in 2-quart saucepan until bacon is crisp. Add enough water, if necessary, to reserved clam liquid to measure 1 cup. Stir clams, liquid, potatoes and pepper into onion mixture. Heat to boiling; reduce heat. Cover and boil until potatoes are tender, about 15 minutes. Stir in milk. Heat, stirring occasionally, just until hot (do not boil). *4 servings.*

Nutrition Information Per Serving

1 serving

Calories	215	Fat, g	6
Protein, g	20	Cholesterol, mg	45
Carbohydrate, g	20	Sodium, mg	200

New England Clam Chowder

Manhattan Clam Chowder

The classic New England Clam Chowder was modified to use tomatoes in place of the cream, and Manhattan Clam Chowder was created.

1/4 cup finely chopped bacon or salt pork

1 small onion, finely chopped (about 1/4 cup)

1 pint shucked fresh clams with liquor*

2 cups finely chopped potatoes

1/3 cup chopped celery

1 cup water

2 teaspoons chopped fresh parsley

1/2 teaspoon salt

1 teaspoon chopped fresh or 1/4 teaspoon dried thyme leaves

1/8 teaspoon pepper

1 can (16 ounces) whole tomatoes, undrained

Cook bacon and onion in Dutch oven, stirring occasionally, until bacon is crisp and onion is tender. Stir clams and clam liquor, potatoes, celery and water into bacon and onion. Heat to boiling; reduce heat. Cover and simmer about 10 minutes or until potatoes are tender. Stir in remaining ingredients. Break up tomatoes. Heat to boiling, stirring occasionally. *5 servings (about 1 1/4 cups each)*

Nutrition Information Per Serving

1 serving

Calories	210	Fat, g	13
Protein, g	7	Cholesterol, mg	15
Carbohydrate, g	17	Sodium, mg	610

*2 cans (6 1/2 ounces each) minced clams, undrained, can be substituted for fresh clams. Stir in clams with remaining ingredients.

2

Country Meats and Mainstays

Americans have always enjoyed hearty main dishes and been quite inventive in using the meats available to create delicious, yet sensible dishes that make the most of the ingredients on hand. Succulent Yankee Pot Roast of Beef grew out of a need to tenderize meat, while satisfying New England Boiled Dinner freed colonial woman to perform their many tasks and not fuss over the stove all day.

Cooks on cattle drives gave us the grilled Texas T-bones, as well as the invention of Chicken-fried Steak to feed hungry cowboys. Ham and Scalloped Potatoes came about as a way to stretch the budget as well as please the taste buds. Macaroni and Cheese, a hit since the time of the American Revolution, and Overnight Lasagne both reflect our love of pasta, as well as convenience.

Most of us have a special spot in our hearts for meat loaf, and you'll find the best recipes here, gathered from all over the country. So perk up your meat loaf tonight with a regional twist, or try one of the other alluring recipes here for a sure-fire main dish.

Yankee Pot Roast of Beef (page 33)

New England Boiled Dinner

Busy colonial women could let corned beef and vegetables simmer all day while they performed their many chores. The result was a hearty and comforting meal, typical of New England cooking. This robust dish was usually served at least once a week, generally with tender corn bread and a generous spoonful of strong, aromatic horseradish. Leftovers were made into red flannel hash for breakfast or eaten cold the following day. Our version doesn't take all day, but it's still a dish that lets you take care of other things while it cooks.

2-pound well-trimmed corned beef boneless brisket or round

1 small onion, cut into fourths

1 clove garlic, crushed

6 small onions

6 medium carrots

3 potatoes, cut in half

3 turnips, cut into fourths

1 small head green cabbage, cut into 6 wedges

Pour enough cold water on corned beef in Dutch oven just to cover. Add 1 small onion, cut into fourths, and the garlic. Heat to boiling; reduce heat. Cover and simmer until beef is almost tender, about 1 hour 40 minutes. Skim fat from broth. Add 6 onions, the carrots, potatoes and turnips. Cover and simmer 20 minutes. Remove beef; keep warm. Add cabbage. Heat to boiling; reduce heat. Simmer uncovered until vegetables are tender, about 15 minutes. *6 servings.*

Nutrition Information Per Serving

1 serving

Calories	420	Fat, g	21
Protein, g	24	Cholesterol, mg	105
Carbohydrate, g	34	Sodium, mg	1300

Chicken-fried Steak

This fried steak and gravy dish, popular in Texas and throughout the Southwest, was invented out of necessity on cattle drives. To feed hungry cowboys, trail cooks would slice beef off a hind quarter, tenderize it by pounding with a meat cleaver, roll in seasoned coating and fry in hot sizzling oil like chicken—hence its name. If you'd like to save a bit of time, substitute tenderized cubed steaks for the round steaks.

1¹/₂ pounds beef boneless round steak, about ¹/₂ inch thick

1 tablespoon water

1 egg

1 cup soda cracker crumbs (about 28 squares)

¹/₄ teaspoon pepper

¹/₄ cup vegetable oil

Milk Gravy (below)

Cut beef steak into 6 serving pieces. Pound each piece until ¹/₄ inch thick to tenderize. Beat water and egg; reserve. Mix cracker crumbs and pepper. Dip beef into egg mixture, then coat with cracker crumbs. Heat oil in 12-inch skillet over medium-high heat until hot. Cook beef in oil, turning once, until brown, 6 to 7 minutes. Remove beef from skillet; keep warm. Reserve drippings for Milk Gravy. Prepare gravy; serve with Chicken-fried Steak. *6 servings.*

MILK GRAVY

¹/₄ cup all-purpose flour

¹/₂ teaspoon salt

2 cups milk

Measure reserved drippings; add enough vegetable oil to drippings, if necessary, to measure ¹/₄ cup. Return drippings to skillet. Stir in flour and salt. Cook over low heat, stirring constantly to loosen brown particles from skillet, until smooth and bubbly; remove from heat. Slowly pour milk into skillet, stirring constantly. Heat to boiling over low heat, stirring constantly. Boil and stir 1 minute.

Nutrition Information Per Serving

1 serving

Calories	340	Fat, g	18
Protein, g	27	Cholesterol, mg	105
Carbohydrate, g	18	Sodium, mg	440

Texas T-bones

In 1854 *Harper's Weekly* reported that the most common meal in America, bar none, was steak. Texas became a prime beef producer with its vast plains and plentiful buffalo grass to nourish sturdy Texas longhorns. Cooking steaks on an open fire was a common practice on Texas cattle drives, one that carried over to our tradition of backyard barbecues. While one T-bone served one person in bygone days, we suggest feeding two people per T-bone.

> *2 beef T-bone steaks, 1¹/₂ inches thick (about 1¹/₂ pounds each)*
>
> *1 clove garlic, cut in half*
>
> *2 teaspoons black peppercorns, crushed*
>
> *¹/₄ cup (¹/₂ stick) margarine or butter, softened*
>
> *1 tablespoon Dijon mustard*
>
> *¹/₂ teaspoon Worcestershire sauce*
>
> *¹/₄ teaspoon lime juice*

Trim fat on beef steaks to ¹/₄-inch thickness. Rub beef with garlic. Press pepper into steaks. Cover and refrigerate 1 hour. Mix margarine, mustard, Worcestershire sauce and lime juice; reserve.

Cover and grill beef 4 to 5 inches from medium heat or coals, about 16 to 18 minutes for medium, turning halfway through cooking. Season after cooking if desired.

Place beef on warm platter; remove bone. Cut beef at slanted angle into thin slices; serve with reserved margarine mixture. *4 servings.*

BROILED T-BONES: Prepare beef as directed. Set oven control to broil. Place beef on rack in broiler pan. Broil beef with tops 3 to 5 inches from heat, until brown, about 35 minutes for medium, turning halfway through cooking. Continue as directed.

Nutrition Information Per Serving

1 serving

Calories	445	Fat, g	27
Protein, g	49	Cholesterol, mg	130
Carbohydrate, g	1	Sodium, mg	300

Texas T-bones

Salisbury Steak

1 pound ground beef

⅓ cup dry bread crumbs

½ teaspoon salt

¼ teaspoon pepper

1 egg

1 large onion, sliced and separated into rings

1 can (10½ ounces) condensed beef broth

8 ounces mushrooms, sliced (about 3 cups)*

2 tablespoons cold water

2 teaspoons cornstarch

Mix ground beef, bread crumbs, salt, pepper and egg; shape into 4 oval patties, each about ¾ inch thick. Cook patties in 10-inch skillet over medium heat, turning occasionally, until brown, about 10 minutes; drain. Add onion, broth and mushrooms. Heat to boiling; reduce heat. Cover and simmer until patties are done, about 10 minutes.

Remove patties; keep warm. Heat onion mixture to boiling. Mix water and cornstarch; stir into onion mixture. Boil and stir 1 minute. Serve over patties. *4 servings.*

Nutrition Information Per Serving

1 serving			
Calories	325	Fat, g	19
Protein, g	25	Cholesterol, mg	120
Carbohydrate, g	13	Sodium, mg	940

*1 can (4 ounces) mushroom stems and pieces, drained, can be substituted for the fresh mushrooms.

Beef and Cabbage Hash

¼ cup (½ stick) margarine or butter

2 cups shredded green cabbage

1 medium onion, chopped (about ½ cup)

2 cups chopped cooked beef

2 cups chopped cooked potatoes (about 2 medium)

½ cup water

2 tablespoons chopped fresh parsley

½ teaspoon salt

⅛ teaspoon pepper

Heat margarine in 10-inch skillet over medium heat. Cook and stir cabbage and onion in margarine until cabbage is crisp-tender, about 2 minutes. Stir in remaining ingredients. Cook uncovered over medium-high heat, without stirring, until liquid is absorbed and bottom is brown, 7 to 9 minutes. *4 servings.*

Nutrition Information Per Serving

1 serving			
Calories	370	Fat, g	25
Protein, g	16	Cholesterol, mg	50
Carbohydrate, g	20	Sodium, mg	890

Favorite Meat Loaf (page 30)

Marvelous Meat Loaves ✫✫✫✫✫✫

Meat loaf is standard family fare across the country. Since the mid-nineteenth century, when veal was the meat most commonly used, families have been sitting down to enjoy this perennial favorite. In the twentieth century, ground beef replaced veal as the meat of choice.

Favorite Meat Loaf

This midwestern meat loaf, seasoned with mustard, pepper and sage, surely upholds country cooking's reputation as hearty and delicious. Soft bread crumbs replace the dry crackers that were typical of the loaves popular at nineteenth-century lunches. Meat loaf is, of course, delicious for dinner, but we suspect that some people bake it just to have the leftovers in a sandwich! Still popular today, meat loaf sandwiches have been popular bring-along lunches since the Industrial Revolution.

1½ pounds ground beef

1 cup milk

1 tablespoon Worcestershire sauce

1 teaspoon salt

½ teaspoon dry mustard

¼ teaspoon pepper

¼ teaspoon rubbed sage

3 slices soft bread, torn into small pieces

1 clove garlic, finely chopped or ⅛ teaspoon garlic powder

1 small onion, chopped (about ¼ cup)

1 egg

½ cup ketchup, chili sauce or barbecue sauce

Heat oven to 350°. Mix all ingredients except ketchup. Spread in ungreased loaf pan, 8½ × 4½ × 2½ or 9 × 5 × 3 inches, or shape into loaf in ungreased rectangular pan, 13 × 9 × 2 inches. Spoon ketchup over top. Bake uncovered until done, 1 to 1¼ hours. Remove from pan. *6 servings.*

INDIVIDUAL MEAT LOAVES: Shape meat mixture into 6 small loaves; place in ungreased rectangular pan, 13 × 9 × 2 inches. Bake as directed—except decrease baking time to 45 minutes.

Nutrition Information Per Serving

1 serving

Calories	330	Fat, g	20
Protein, g	22	Cholesterol, mg	105
Carbohydrate, g	15	Sodium, mg	780

Old-fashioned Meat Loaf

On the East Coast, rolled oat flakes were the secret ingredient of the perfect meat loaf. While some call oats or bread a "stretcher," in fact, they serve to bind the meat mixture into a loaf of wonderful texture and juiciness. Tomatoes, tomato sauce and ketchup are often added to contribute moisture as well as flavor. A number of cooks believed that using beef alone makes for a dry meat loaf, so our Old-fashioned Meat Loaf uses rolled oats and a mixture of ground pork and beef. While some cooks feel that there is no end to the number of ingredients that can go into a meat loaf, this recipe takes a simpler approach.

1 can (16 ounces) whole tomatoes
1¹/₄ pounds ground beef
¹/₄ pound ground pork
³/₄ cup regular oats
¹/₃ cup chopped onion
1 egg
1 teaspoon salt
¹/₄ teaspoon pepper

Heat oven to 375°. Drain tomatoes, reserving ¹/₄ cup liquid. Cut tomatoes up with fork. Mix reserved liquid, the tomatoes and remaining ingredients thoroughly. Pack in loaf pan, 8¹/₂ × 4¹/₂ × 2¹/₂ inches. Bake uncovered until done, 1 to 1¹/₄ hours. Remove from pan. *6 servings.*

Nutrition Information Per Serving

1 serving

Calories	310	Fat, g	20
Protein, g	22	Cholesterol, mg	105
Carbohydrate, g	11	Sodium, mg	550

Western Meat Loaf

Different regions of our country each give us a special twist to classic recipes. Crops, weather, ethnicity of the people and tradition play significant roles in determining a certain region's take on a recipe. On the American frontier, for example, cooks learned to use easily grown horseradish to season their meat loaves. They dug up horseradish roots, replanted the tops in the ground, and ground the root to use in cooking. With the pungent flavor of horseradish and dry mustard, our Western Meat Loaf recipe reflects its frontier heritage. This hearty meaty loaf has been a favorite of western ranch hands through the years.

1 can (8 ounces) tomato sauce
1¹/₂ pounds ground beef
¹/₂ pound ground pork
2 cups soft bread crumbs
2 to 4 tablespoons prepared horseradish
1 teaspoon dry mustard
¹/₂ teaspoon salt
¹/₄ teaspoon pepper
1 medium onion, finely chopped (about ¹/₂ cup)
2 eggs, slightly beaten
1 tablespoon packed brown sugar
¹/₄ teaspoon dry mustard

Heat oven to 350°. Reserve ¹/₄ cup of the tomato sauce. Mix the remaining tomato sauce and remaining ingredients except brown sugar and ¹/₄ teaspoon dry mustard. Spread in ungreased loaf pan, 8¹/₂ × 4¹/₂ × 2¹/₂ or 9 × 5 × 3 inches, or shape mixture into loaf in ungreased rectangular pan, 13 × 9 × 2 inches.

Mix reserved tomato sauce, brown sugar and ¹/₄ teaspoon dry mustard; spread over loaf. Bake uncovered until done, 1 to 1¹/₄ hours. Cover loosely with aluminum foil; let stand 10 minutes. Remove from pan. *8 servings.*

Nutrition Information Per Serving

1 serving

Calories	380	Fat, g	20
Protein, g	26	Cholesterol, mg	120
Carbohydrate, g	24	Sodium, mg	555

Overnight Lasagne

Lasagne is an American favorite, always perfect for family meals, casual get-togethers and potluck suppers. While Americans use the word *lasagne* to mean a casserole made with lasagne noodles, cheese and tomato sauce, Italians use it to mean the wide noodles used in many kinds of Italian dishes.

1 pound ground beef

1 medium onion, chopped (about ½ cup)

1 clove garlic, crushed

⅓ cup chopped fresh or 2 tablespoons dried parsley leaves

1 tablespoon sugar

2 tablespoons chopped fresh or 1½ teaspoons dried basil leaves

1 teaspoon seasoned salt

1 can (16 ounces) whole tomatoes, undrained

1 can (10¾ ounces) condensed tomato soup

1 can (6 ounces) tomato paste

2½ cups water

12 uncooked lasagne noodles (about 12 ounces)

1 container (12 ounces) creamed cottage cheese

2 cups shredded mozzarella cheese (8 ounces)

¼ cup grated Parmesan cheese

Cook and stir ground beef, onion and garlic in Dutch oven until beef is brown; drain. Stir in parsley, sugar, basil, seasoned salt, tomatoes, tomato soup, tomato paste and water; break up tomatoes. Heat to boiling, stirring occasionally; reduce heat. Simmer uncovered 20 minutes.

Spread 2 cups of the sauce mixture in ungreased rectangular baking dish, 13 × 9 × 2 inches. Top with 4 noodles. Spread half of the cottage cheese over noodles; spread with 2 cups of the sauce mixture. Sprinkle with 1 cup of the mozzarella cheese. Repeat with 4 noodles, the remaining cottage cheese, 2 cups of the sauce mixture and the remaining mozzarella cheese. Top with the remaining noodles and sauce mixture; sprinkle with Parmesan cheese. Cover and refrigerate up to 12 hours.

Heat oven to 350°. Bake covered 30 minutes. Uncover and bake until hot and bubbly, 30 to 40 minutes longer. Let stand 15 minutes before cutting. *8 servings.*

EASY OVERNIGHT LASAGNE: Substitute 6½ cups prepared spaghetti sauce for the parsley, sugar, basil, seasoned salt, canned tomatoes, tomato soup, tomato paste and water. Stir sauce into drained beef mixture. Do not simmer. Continue as directed.

Nutrition Information Per Serving

1 serving

Calories	420	Fat, g	18
Protein, g	30	Cholesterol, mg	80
Carbohydrate, g	35	Sodium, mg	1100

Yankee Pot Roast of Beef

In colonial days it wasn't always easy to find tender beef. To tenderize their meat, settlers placed it in a tightly covered pot and simmered it for several hours, letting the low, moist heat work its magic. If a tight lid wasn't available, cooks sealed the pot with pastry around the rim to ensure a tight fit. Root vegetables, easy to store year round, were a pleasing addition to this meal in a pot.

¹/₄ cup all-purpose flour

2 teaspoons salt

¹/₂ teaspoon pepper

4- to 5-pound boneless beef shoulder pot roast

1 tablespoon shortening

¹/₂ cup water

4 medium stalks celery cut into fourths

4 medium carrots cut into fourths

3 medium potatoes, cut into 1¹/₂-inch pieces

2 medium rutabagas or yellow turnips cut into 1¹/₂-inch pieces

1 large onion, chopped (about 1 cup)

Mix flour, salt and pepper; rub over pot roast. Heat shortening in 12-inch skillet or Dutch oven until melted; brown beef on all sides. Drain fat from skillet; add water. Heat to boiling; reduce heat. Cover tightly and simmer on top of range or cook in 325° oven 2 hours.

Arrange vegetables around beef. Add ¹/₄ cup water if necessary. Cover and simmer, stirring vegetables occasionally, until beef and vegetables are tender, 45 minutes to 1 hour. Remove beef and vegetables from skillet. Skim fat from broth; serve broth with beef. *12 servings.*

Nutrition Information Per Serving

1 serving

Calories	430	Fat, g	24
Protein, g	41	Cholesterol, mg	120
Carbohydrate, g	12	Sodium, mg	480

Texas Chili

3 pounds beef boneless round steak, cut
  into 1/2-inch cubes

3 tablespoons vegetable oil

1/2 cup chopped fresh parsley

4 cups water

3 tablespoons chopped fresh or 1 tablespoon dried oregano leaves

1 tablespoon paprika

2 teaspoons ground cumin

1 1/2 teaspoons salt

1 to 2 teaspoons crushed red pepper

3/4 teaspoon ground coriander

1 large bay leaf

3 large cloves garlic, crushed

1 large onion, chopped (about 1 cup)

1 can (8 ounces) tomato sauce

1 cup shredded Cheddar or Monterey
  Jack cheese (4 ounces)

1 cup sour cream

1 medium avocado, chopped

Cook and stir half of the beef at a time in oil in Dutch oven over medium heat until light brown. Stir in parsley, water, seasonings, garlic, onion and tomato sauce. Heat to boiling; reduce heat. Cover and simmer 1 hour, stirring occasionally. Uncover and simmer, stirring occasionally, until mixture thickens, about 1 1/2 hours longer. Remove bay leaf. Serve with cheese, sour cream and avocado. *5 servings.*

CHILI WITH BEANS: Substitute 3 pounds ground beef for the beef stock. Omit oil. Cook and stir ground beef until brown; drain. Continue as directed. After removing bay leaf, stir in 3 cans (15 ounces each) pinto beans, undrained; heat to boiling. *8 servings.*

Nutrition Information Per Serving

1 serving

Calories	395	Fat, g	24
Protein, g	37	Cholesterol, mg	120
Carbohydrate, g	8	Sodium, mg	740

Lamb Barbecue

4- to 5-pound leg of lamb, boned

2 small cloves garlic, slivered

1/3 cup packed brown sugar

1/3 cup vegetable oil

1/2 cup red wine vinegar

2 tablespoons dried tarragon leaves

1 teaspoon salt

2 green onions, cut into 2-inch slices

1 can (8 ounces) tomato sauce

Trim excess fat from lamb; if necessary, cut lamb to lie flat. Cut 4 or 5 slits in lamb with tip of sharp knife; insert garlic slivers in slits. Place lamb in shallow glass or plastic bowl. Mix remaining ingredients except tomato sauce; pour over lamb. Cover and refrigerate at least 8 hours, turning lamb 2 or 3 times.

Remove lamb from marinade; stir tomato sauce into marinade. Cover and grill lamb 5 to 6 inches from medium coals, turning every 10 minutes, until done (meat thermometer registers 175°), 50 to 60 minutes; brush 2 or 3 times with marinade during last 10 minutes of grilling. Remove garlic slivers before serving. *14 servings.*

Nutrition Information Per Serving

1 serving

Calories	330	Fat, g	17
Protein, g	37	Cholesterol, mg	120
Carbohydrate, g	7	Sodium, mg	340

Texas Chili

Venison Stew

4 slices bacon, cut into ½-inch pieces

1 pound boneless venison, cut into 1-inch cubes

2 cups water

1 cup dry red wine or beef broth

¾ teaspoon chopped fresh or ¼ teaspoon dried thyme leaves

¾ teaspoon chopped fresh or ¼ teaspoon dried marjoram leaves

½ teaspoon salt

¼ teaspoon pepper

4 ounces tiny pearl onions (about 1 cup)

2 medium carrots, cut into 1-inch pieces

1 large potato, cut into 1-inch pieces

½ cup cold water

3 tablespoons all-purpose flour

½ teaspoon browning sauce, if desired

2 tablespoons chopped fresh parsley

Cook bacon in Dutch oven, stirring occasionally, until crisp. Remove bacon with slotted spoon; reserve. Cook and stir venison in bacon fat until brown, about 7 minutes. Add 2 cups water, the wine, thyme, marjoram, salt and pepper. Heat to boiling; reduce heat. Cover and simmer until venison is almost tender, about 2 hours.

Stir in onions, carrots and potato. Heat to boiling; reduce heat. Cover and simmer until vegetables are tender, about 30 minutes. Shake ½ cup cold water and the flour in tightly covered container; gradually stir into stew. Stir in browning sauce. Heat to boiling, stirring constantly. Boil and stir 1 minute. Sprinkle with bacon and parsley. *5 servings.*

BEEF STEW: Substitute 1 pound beef for the venison.

Nutrition Information Per Serving

1 serving

Calories	210	Fat, g	5
Protein, g	23	Cholesterol, mg	80
Carbohydrate, g	15	Sodium, mg	350

Stuffed Crown Roast of Pork

This special recipe from pig-farming country on the Minnesota-Iowa border adds to the Midwest's well-earned reputation for good home cooking. It's a delicious choice for special-occasion dinner parties such as anniversary celebrations. The hearty apple, walnut and bread stuffing and rich Pan Gravy perfectly complement this wonderful roast.

8-pound pork crown roast

2 teaspoons seasoned salt

1/2 teaspoon pepper

1/2 teaspoon dry mustard

1 medium stalk celery, chopped (about 1/2 cup)

1 medium onion, finely chopped (about 1/2 cup)

1/2 cup chopped walnuts

1/4 cup (1/2 stick) plus 2 tablespoons margarine or butter

2 cups chopped pared or unpared cooking apples

2 tablespoons sugar

3 cups soft bread cubes

1/4 cup chopped fresh parsley

1/2 teaspoon ground sage

2 teaspoons chopped fresh or 1/2 teaspoon dried thyme leaves

1/4 teaspoon ground nutmeg

Spiced crabapples or paper frills, if desired

Pan Gravy (below)

Heat oven to 325°. Place pork roast, bone ends up, on rack in shallow roasting pan. Mix seasoned salt, pepper and mustard; sprinkle over pork. Wrap bone ends in aluminum foil to pre-vent excessive browning. Insert meat thermometer so tip is in center of thickest part of pork and does not touch bone or rest in fat. Roast uncovered 1 1/2 hours.

Cook and stir celery, onion and walnuts in margarine in Dutch oven or 12-inch skillet until onion is tender. Stir in apples and sugar. Cook and stir until apples soften, 3 to 5 minutes; remove from heat. Stir in bread cubes, parsley, sage, thyme and nutmeg.

Fill center of pork roast with stuffing mixture. Roast uncovered until meat thermometer registers 155°, about 2 to 2 1/2 hours longer. (Allow 20 to 25 minutes per pound total cooking time.) Cover with foil if top becomes too brown. Remove roast from oven; cover with aluminum foil tent. Let stand 15 minutes; temperature will rise to 160°. Remove roast to serving platter; keep warm. Prepare Pan Gravy. Just before serving, cover bone ends with spiced crabapples or paper frills, if desired. *14 servings*.

PAN GRAVY

1/4 cup all-purpose flour
Water or chicken broth

Strain pork drippings into bowl. Let fat rise to top of drippings; skim off fat, reserving 1/4 cup. Add enough water to drippings to measure 2 cups; reserve. Stir flour into reserved 1/4 cup fat in 2-quart saucepan. Cook over medium heat, stirring constantly, until smooth and bubbly; remove from heat. Stir in reserved drippings. Heat to boiling, stirring constantly. Boil and stir 1 minute. Serve gravy with roast.

Nutrition Information Per Serving

1 serving			
Calories	745	Fat, g	44
Protein, g	71	Cholesterol, mg	235
Carbohydrate, g	16	Sodium, mg	470

Fruit-stuffed Pork Roast

¹/₂ teaspoon ground cinnamon

¹/₄ teaspoon ground cloves

15 dried apricot halves (about 3 ounces)

9 pitted prunes (about 3 ounces)

4-pound pork boneless top loin roast (double)

³/₄ teaspoon salt

¹/₄ teaspoon pepper

1¹/₄ cups apple cider or juice

1 tablespoon cornstarch

1 tablespoon cold water

Sprinkle cinnamon and cloves over apricots and prunes; toss to coat. Stuff fruit lengthwise between the 2 pieces of pork roast in ribbon about 2 inches wide (work from both ends of roast). Sprinkle with salt and pepper.

Heat oven to 325°. Place pork, fat side up, on rack in shallow roasting pan. Insert meat thermometer so tip is in center of thickest part of pork and does not rest in fat or fruit mixture. Roast uncovered until thermometer registers 170°, about 3 hours. After 1¹/₂ hours, brush occasionally with ¹/₄ cup of the apple cider.

Remove pork and rack from pan; keep pork warm. Pour remaining cider into roasting pan; stir to loosen brown particles. Mix cornstarch and water; stir into cider mixture. Heat to boiling, stirring constantly. Boil and stir 1 minute. Serve with pork. *12 servings.*

Nutrition Information Per Serving

1 serving

Calories	405	Fat, g	21
Protein, g	41	Cholesterol, mg	135
Carbohydrate, g	13	Sodium, mg	240

Fruit-stuffed Pork Roast

Stuffed Pork Chops

¹/₃ cup chopped celery (with leaves)

3 tablespoons finely chopped onion

¹/₄ cup (¹/₂ stick) margarine or butter

2¹/₄ cups soft bread cubes (about 4 slices bread)

¹/₂ teaspoon salt

¹/₄ teaspoon rubbed sage

³/₄ teaspoon chopped fresh or ¹/₄ teaspoon dried thyme leaves

¹/₈ teaspoon pepper

4 pork loin chops, about 1 inch thick (with pockets cut into chops)

2 tablespoons vegetable oil

¹/₄ cup apple cider or juice

Cook and stir celery and onion in margarine in 2-quart saucepan over medium heat, stirring frequently, until celery is tender; remove from heat. Stir in bread cubes, salt, sage, thyme and pepper.

Stuff each pork chop pocket with about ¹/₃ cup of the bread mixture. Fasten by inserting 2 toothpicks in X shape through edges of pork. Fry in oil in 10-inch skillet over medium heat until brown on both sides, about 15 minutes; drain. Add apple cider; reduce heat. Cover and simmer until pork chops are done, about 1 hour. Remove toothpicks. *4 servings.*

Nutrition Information Per Serving

1 serving

Calories	395	Fat, g	28
Protein, g	20	Cholesterol, mg	60
Carbohydrate, g	16	Sodium, mg	580

Glazed Baked Ham

¹/₄ cup packed brown sugar

¹/₄ teaspoon ground cloves

¹/₄ teaspoon ground cinnamon

1 can (6 ounces) frozen orange juice concentrate, thawed

5- to 7-pound fully cooked smoked ham

Whole cloves, if desired

Orange slices, if desired

Cranberry Sauce or Raisin Sauce (below)

Heat oven to 325°. Mix brown sugar, cloves, cinnamon and orange juice concentrate. Place ham, fat side up, on rack in shallow roasting pan. Insert meat thermometer so tip is in thickest part of ham and does not touch bone or rest in fat. Spoon or spread half of the juice mixture onto ham. Roast uncovered until meat thermometer registers 135°, 1¹/₂ to 2 hours.

About 30 minutes before ham is done, remove from oven; pour drippings from pan. Cut fat surface of ham in uniform diamond pattern ¹/₄ inch deep. Insert whole clove in each diamond, if desired. Spoon or spread remaining juice mixture on ham; continue baking 30 minutes. Remove from oven. Cover and let stand 10 minutes. Garnish with orange slices, if desired. Serve with Cranberry Sauce. *10 servings*.

CRANBERRY SAUCE

1 can (16 ounces) whole berry cranberry sauce

1 teaspoon grated orange peel

¹/₂ teaspoon ground ginger

¹/₄ teaspoon ground allspice

Heat all ingredients until hot, stirring occasionally. Serve warm.

RAISIN SAUCE

2 cups apple cider or juice

3 tablespoons cornstarch

1 cup raisins

2 tablespoons margarine or butter

Gradually stir apple cider into cornstarch in 1-quart saucepan. Add raisins and margarine. Heat over medium heat, stirring constantly, until mixture thickens and boils. Boil and stir 1 minute. Serve warm.

Nutrition Information Per Serving

1 serving

Calories	445	Fat, g	13
Protein, g	48	Cholesterol, mg	120
Carbohydrate, g	34	Sodium, mg	2740

Ham and Scalloped Potatoes

Resourceful farm women found this recipe to be a thrifty way to stretch the meat budget. You'll find that combining leftover ham; sliced potatoes; and a rich, creamy sauce still makes for a hearty, no-fuss meal—perfect for family dinners, church suppers and even barn raisings!

3 tablespoons margarine or butter

3 tablespoons all-purpose flour

¹/₂ teaspoon salt

¹/₄ teaspoon pepper

2¹/₂ cups milk

2 tablespoons chopped fresh parsley

6 medium potatoes (about 2 pounds), thinly sliced (about 4 cups)

1 small onion, finely chopped (about ¹/₄ cup)

1¹/₂ cups cubed fully cooked smoked ham

1 tablespoon margarine or butter

Heat 3 tablespoons margarine in 1¹/₂-quart saucepan over low heat until melted. Stir in flour, salt and pepper. Cook over low heat, stirring constantly, until smooth and bubbly; remove from heat. Stir in milk. Heat to boiling, stirring constantly. Boil and stir 1 minute. Stir in parsley.

Heat oven to 350°. Grease 2-quart casserole. Layer one-third of the potatoes, one-half of the onion and ham and one-third of the white sauce in casserole; repeat. Top with remaining potatoes and sauce. Dot with 1 tablespoon margarine. Cover and bake 30 minutes. Uncover and bake until potatoes are tender, 60 to 70 minutes longer. Let stand 5 to 10 minutes before serving. *6 servings*.

Nutrition Information Per Serving

1 serving

Calories	305	Fat, g	13
Protein, g	14	Cholesterol, mg	30
Carbohydrate, g	33	Sodium, mg	860

Sausage Pie

1¹/₂ pounds bulk pork sausage

1 medium onion, chopped (about ¹/₂ cup)

1 tablespoon sugar

1¹/₂ teaspoons salt

1 medium head green cabbage (1³/₄ pounds), cut into large chunks and cored

1 can (16 ounces) whole tomatoes, undrained

Pastry for 9-inch one-crust pie (see page 102)

2 tablespoons all-purpose flour

¹/₄ cup cold water

Cook and stir sausage and onion in Dutch oven until sausage is done; drain. Stir in sugar, salt, cabbage and tomatoes. Heat to boiling; reduce heat. Cover and simmer 10 minutes.

Heat oven to 400°. Prepare pastry; shape into flattened round on lightly floured cloth-covered board. Roll to fit top of 2-quart casserole. Fold into fourths; cut slits so steam can escape.

Mix flour and water; stir into hot sausage mixture. Pour into ungreased casserole. Place pastry over top and unfold; seal pastry to edge of casserole. Bake until crust is brown, 25 to 30 minutes. *6 servings.*

Nutrition Information Per Serving

1 serving

Calories	430	Fat, g	28
Protein, g	15	Cholesterol, mg	45
Carbohydrate, g	30	Sodium, mg	1570

Sausage Pie

Sausage and Bean Casserole

1 package (10 ounces) frozen lima beans

1 can (21 ounces) baked beans

1 can (15¹/₂ ounces) kidney beans, drained

¹/₂ pound Italian or pork link sausages

¹/₂ cup ketchup

1 tablespoon packed brown sugar

¹/₂ teaspoon salt

¹/₂ teaspoon dry mustard

¹/₈ teaspoon pepper

1 small onion, chopped (about ¹/₄ cup)

Heat oven to 400°. Cook lima beans as directed on package; drain. Mix lima beans, baked beans and kidney beans in ungreased 2-quart casserole. Heat sausages and small amount of water to boiling; reduce heat. Cover and simmer 5 minutes; drain. Cook sausages until brown on all sides (do not prick sausages). Cut each sausage into 2 or 3 pieces; stir into beans. Mix remaining ingredients; stir into bean mixture. Bake uncovered until hot and bubbly, 40 to 50 minutes. *6 servings.*

HAM AND BEAN CASSEROLE: Substitute ³/₄ cup cut-up fully cooked smoked ham for the cooked sausages.

Nutrition Information Per Serving

1 serving

Calories	420	Fat, g	12
Protein, g	22	Cholesterol, mg	35
Carbohydrate, g	56	Sodium, mg	1300

Barbecued Spareribs

4¹/₂-pound rack fresh pork loin back ribs

3 cups water

Tomato Barbecue Sauce or Spicy Barbecue Sauce (below)

Place pork ribs in Dutch oven; add water. Heat to boiling; reduce heat. Cover and simmer 5 minutes; drain.

Cover and grill pork 5 to 6 inches from medium coals, brushing with Tomato Barbecue Sauce every 3 minutes, until done and meat begins to pull away from bones (meat thermometer registers 170°), 15 to 20 minutes. Heat remaining sauce to boiling; serve with ribs. *6 servings.*

TOMATO BARBECUE SAUCE

²/₃ cup ketchup
¹/₃ cup water
¹/₄ cup (¹/₂ stick) margarine or butter
1 tablespoon dry mustard
2 tablespoons Worcestershire sauce
¹/₂ teaspoon garlic powder
¹/₄ teaspoon red pepper sauce
1 small onion, chopped (about ¹/₄ cup), or 1 teaspoon onion powder

Heat all ingredients, stirring frequently, until margarine is melted.

SPICY BARBECUE SAUCE

¹/₃ cup margarine or butter
2 tablespoons vinegar
2 tablespoons water
1 teaspoon sugar
¹/₂ teaspoon garlic powder
¹/₂ teaspoon onion powder
¹/₂ teaspoon pepper
Dash of ground red pepper (cayenne)

Heat all ingredients, stirring frequently, until margarine is melted.

OVEN BARBECUED SPARERIBS: Do not boil ribs; cut into serving pieces and place, meaty sides up, on rack in shallow roasting pan. Roast uncovered in 325° oven 1¹/₂ hours. Brush with sauce. Roast, turning and brushing frequently with sauce, until done, about 45 minutes longer.

Nutrition Information Per Serving

1 serving

Calories	560	Fat, g	46
Protein, g	27	Cholesterol, mg	110
Carbohydrate, g	9	Sodium, mg	530

Macaroni and Cheese

1 to 1¹/₂ cups uncooked elbow macaroni (about 6 ounces)

¹/₄ cup (¹/₂ stick) margarine or butter

¹/₂ teaspoon salt

¹/₄ teaspoon pepper

1 small onion, chopped (about ¹/₄ cup)

¹/₄ cup all-purpose flour

1³/₄ cups milk

8 ounces process American loaf or sharp process American cheese loaf or process cheese spread loaf, cut into ¹/₂-inch cubes

Heat oven to 375°. Cook macaroni as directed on package; drain. Cook and stir margarine, salt, pepper and onion in 2-quart saucepan over medium heat until onion is slightly tender. Stir in flour. Cook over low heat, stirring constantly, until smooth and bubbly; remove from heat. Stir in milk. Heat to boiling, stirring constantly. Boil and stir 1 minute; remove from heat. Stir in cheese until melted. Mix macaroni and cheese sauce in ungreased ¹/₂-quart casserole. Bake uncovered 30 minutes. *5 servings.*

TOMATO MACARONI AND CHEESE: Mix ¹/₄ cup sliced ripe olives into cheese sauce. Arrange 1 large tomato, cut into 5 slices, around edge of casserole before baking.

Nutrition Information Per Serving

1 serving

Calories	320	Fat, g	18
Protein, g	13	Cholesterol, mg	35
Carbohydrate, g	27	Sodium, mg	720

New Hampshire Cheese Soup

1 large potato, chopped (about 1¹/₂ cups)

1 large onion, finely chopped (about 1 cup)

1 small carrot, finely chopped (about ¹/₄ cup)

1 small stalk celery, thinly sliced (about ¹/₄ cup)

1 cup water

1 cup shredded sharp Cheddar cheese (4 ounces)

2 cups chicken broth

¹/₂ cup half-and-half

2 tablespoons chopped fresh parsley

Heat potato, onion, carrot, celery and water to boiling in 2-quart saucepan; reduce heat. Cover and simmer until vegetables are tender, 10 to 15 minutes. Stir in cheese, broth and half-and-half; heat through. Sprinkle with parsley. *4 servings.*

Nutrition Information Per Serving

1 serving

Calories	220	Fat, g	14
Protein, g	11	Cholesterol, mg	40
Carbohydrate, g	13	Sodium, mg	590

Minnesota Wild Rice Soup

Native Americans in the upper Midwest called wild rice *mahnomen*, or "precious grain." This delicacy isn't actually rice but is a grain from an aquatic plant. Minnesotan cooks have used this native plant in many recipes, this creamy, chowderlike soup being one of the more popular creations.

2 medium stalks celery, sliced (about 1 cup)

1 medium carrot, coarsely shredded (about ¹/₂ cup)

1 medium onion, chopped (about ¹/₂ cup)

1 small green bell pepper, chopped (about ¹/₂ cup)

2 tablespoons margarine or butter

3 tablespoons all-purpose flour

1 teaspoon salt

¹/₄ teaspoon pepper

1¹/₂ cups cooked wild rice

1 cup water

1 can (10¹/₂ ounces) condensed chicken broth

1 cup half-and-half

¹/₃ cup slivered almonds, toasted

¹/₄ cup chopped fresh parsley

Cook and stir celery, carrot, onion and bell pepper in margarine in 3-quart saucepan until celery is tender, about 5 minutes. Stir in flour, salt and pepper. Stir in wild rice, water and broth. Heat to boiling; reduce heat. Cover and simmer 15 minutes, stirring occasionally. Stir in remaining ingredients. Heat just until hot (do not boil). *5 servings.*

Nutrition Information Per Serving

1 serving

Calories	260	Fat, g	15
Protein, g	8	Cholesterol, mg	20
Carbohydrate, g	23	Sodium, mg	910

Minnesota Wild Rice Soup and Brown Bread
(page 73)

3

Fresh from the Garden

Americans love fresh produce, and early settlers grew just about all the vegetables they ate. This bounty made for wonderful vegetable dishes and salads in season. Today, we are able to enjoy almost all of these dishes throughout the year. Hearty Farm-fried Potatoes, soothing Corn Pudding and zesty Country-fried Cabbage were all staples on farm tables. And other fresh treats, such as spicy Stuffed Zucchini, crunchy Pacific Green Beans and pretty Corn and Pepper Cakes will be a welcome addition to any table!

Fresh salads were also in abundance on the farm, direct from kitchen gardens close to the house. Zesty Wilted Spinach Salad and Country Potato Salad rounded out many a farmer's meal, while coleslaw was also a traditional favorite. There are many versions of this crunchy, satisfying salad, and we have brought the best recipes to you: a tangy Texas coleslaw, a salad from Pennsylvania Dutch country and a New England version with its own boiled dressing.

Stuffed Zucchini (page 50)

Stuffed Zucchini

4 medium zucchini (about 2 pounds)

1 medium onion, chopped (about ¹/₂ cup)

¹/₄ cup (¹/₂ stick) margarine or butter

1 can (4 ounces) chopped green chilies, drained

1 jar (2 ounces) diced pimientos, drained

1¹/₂ cups herb-seasoned stuffing mix (dry)

³/₄ cup shredded mozzarella or Monterey Jack cheese

Heat 2 inches water (salted if desired) to boiling. Add zucchini. Heat to boiling; reduce heat. Cover and simmer just until tender, 8 to 10 minutes; drain. Cool slightly; cut each zucchini lengthwise in half. Spoon out pulp; chop coarsely. Place zucchini, cut sides up, in ungreased baking dish, 13 × 9 × 2 inches.

Heat oven to 350°. Cook and stir onion in margarine in 10-inch skillet until onion is tender. Stir in chopped pulp, chilies, pimientos and stuffing mix. Divide stuffing mixture among zucchini halves. Sprinkle each with about 1 tablespoon cheese. Bake uncovered until hot, 30 to 35 minutes. *8 servings.*

Nutrition Information Per Serving

1 serving

Calories	140	Fat, g	9
Protein, g	5	Cholesterol, mg	5
Carbohydrate, g	10	Sodium, mg	380

Country-fried Cabbage

This quick-and-easy recipe was a specialty of Eastern European immigrants to this country. Just as potatoes are the classic accompaniment to meat in the United States, so is cabbage the traditional side dish for meat in Europe. Recipes using red cabbage are most closely associated with the cooking of German immigrants. This dish is often served in late summer or fall when the large leafy heads of cabbage are harvested.

2 tablespoons bacon fat or vegetable oil

1¹/₂ pounds green or red cabbage, shredded (about 9 cups)

2 tablespoons whipping (heavy) cream

1¹/₂ teaspoons lemon juice or vinegar

Salt and pepper

Heat bacon fat in 10-inch skillet. Add cabbage. Cook over low heat, stirring frequently, until light brown. Cover and cook, stirring occasionally, until crisp-tender, about 5 minutes. Stir in whipping cream and lemon juice; heat until whipping cream is hot. Sprinkle with salt and pepper. *4 servings.*

Nutrition Information Per Serving

1 serving

Calories	125	Fat, g	7
Protein, g	3	Cholesterol, mg	15
Carbohydrate, g	13	Sodium, mg	370

Pacific Green Beans

Herbs grow in abundance in the mild climate of the Pacific Northwest. Summer savory, with its peppery flavor, is often served there with mild green beans. While the old-fashioned southern method is to cook green beans to an olive green color and a tender texture, in the Northwest, they're cooked just until crisp-tender and still bright green.

1 pound fresh green beans

1 small onion, finely chopped (about ¼ cup)

1 tablespoon margarine, butter or bacon fat

¼ cup water

¼ teaspoon salt

2 teaspoons chopped fresh or ½ teaspoon dried summer savory leaves

1 tablespoon chopped fresh parsley

Cut beans into 1½-inch pieces or leave whole. Cook and stir onion in margarine in 3-quart saucepan over medium heat until onion is tender. Stir in beans, water and salt. Heat to boiling; reduce heat. Cover and simmer, stirring occasionally, until beans are crisp-tender, 10 to 13 minutes for pieces, 13 to 16 minutes for whole beans. Stir in summer savory and parsley. *5 servings.*

Nutrition Information Per Serving

1 serving

Calories	40	Fat, g	2
Protein, g	1	Cholesterol, mg	0
Carbohydrate, g	5	Sodium, mg	140

Skillet Acorn Squash

1 large acorn squash (about 2 pounds)
1/4 cup pecan pieces
1/2 cup orange juice
2 tablespoons packed brown sugar
1 tablespoon margarine or butter
1/4 teaspoon ground cinnamon

Cut squash lengthwise in half; remove seeds and fibers. Cut each half crosswise into 1/2-inch slices.

Heat pecans in 12-inch skillet over medium heat, stirring constantly, until lightly browned; remove from skillet. Mix orange juice, brown sugar, margarine and cinnamon in skillet. Stir in squash. Heat to boiling; reduce heat. Cover and simmer 10 minutes; turn squash. Cover and simmer until squash is tender, 5 to 8 minutes. Sprinkle with pecans. *4 servings.*

Nutrition Information Per Serving

1 serving

Calories	170	Fat, g	9
Protein, g	1	Cholesterol, mg	0
Carbohydrate, g	21	Sodium, mg	35

Skillet Acorn Squash

Corn Pudding

Corn on the cob is a time-honored American favorite. And corn off the cob can be just as wonderful! In the summer, use just-picked corn to make this simple and creamy pudding. Be sure to scrape all the pulp and milk from the cob.

4 medium ears corn*
2 tablespoons sugar
2 tablespoons all-purpose flour
1/2 teaspoon salt
Dash of pepper
2 eggs
1 1/4 cups milk
2 tablespoons margarine or butter, melted
1/2 teaspoon ground nutmeg

Heat oven to 350°. Grease 1-quart casserole or soufflé dish. Cut enough kernels from corn to measure 2 cups. (Scrape ears with knife to extract all pulp and milk.) Mix the corn, sugar, flour, salt and pepper in 2-quart bowl. Stir in eggs. Stir in milk and margarine; pour into casserole. Sprinkle with nutmeg.

Set casserole in baking pan on middle oven rack. Pour hot water into pan until about 1 1/2 inches deep. Bake until knife inserted halfway between center and edge comes out clean, about 50 to 55 minutes. *8 servings.*

Nutrition Information Per Serving

1 serving

Calories	125	Fat, g	5
Protein, g	4	Cholesterol, mg	55
Carbohydrate, g	16	Sodium, mg	210

*2 cups frozen whole kernel corn, thawed, or 1 can (16 ounces) whole kernel corn, drained, can be substituted for the fresh corn.

Corn and Pepper Cakes

4 medium ears corn*

¹/₂ cup all-purpose flour

¹/₄ cup milk

1 tablespoon sugar

¹/₂ teaspoon salt

¹/₈ teaspoon pepper

2 egg yolks

1 small bell pepper, finely chopped (about ¹/₂ cup)

2 egg whites

¹/₂ cup vegetable oil

Cut enough kernels from corn to measure 2 cups (scrape ears with knife to extract all pulp and milk). Beat flour, milk, sugar, salt, pepper and egg yolks in medium bowl. Stir in corn and bell pepper. Beat egg whites until stiff and glossy. Fold corn mixture into egg whites.

Heat oil in 10-inch skillet. Drop corn mixture by tablespoonfuls into hot oil. Fry about 30 seconds on each side or until golden brown. Serve with sour cream if desired. *6 servings.*

Nutrition Information Per Serving

1 serving

Calories	305	Fat, g	21
Protein, g	5	Cholesterol, mg	70
Carbohydrate, g	24	Sodium, mg	210

*1 package (10 ounces) frozen whole kernel corn, cooked, can be substituted for the fresh corn.

Cheesy Grits

2 cups milk

2 cups water

1 teaspoon salt

¹/₄ teaspoon pepper

1 cup hominy quick grits

1¹/₂ cups shredded Cheddar cheese (6 ounces)

¹/₄ cup sliced green onions

2 eggs, slightly beaten

1 tablespoon margarine or butter

¹/₄ teaspoon paprika

Heat oven to 350°. Grease 1¹/₂-quart casserole. Heat milk, water, salt and pepper to boiling in 2-quart saucepan. Gradually add grits, stirring constantly; reduce heat. Simmer uncovered, stirring frequently, until thick, about 5 minutes. Stir in cheese and onions. Stir 1 cup of the hot mixture into eggs; stir into remaining hot mixture in saucepan.

Pour hot mixture into casserole. Dot with margarine; sprinkle with paprika. Bake uncovered until set, 35 to 40 minutes. Let stand 10 minutes. *8 servings.*

Nutrition Information Per Serving

1 serving

Calories	210	Fat, g	11
Protein, g	10	Cholesterol, mg	80
Carbohydrate, g	18	Sodium, mg	460

Corn and Pepper Cakes and Corn Pudding (page 53)

Crunchy Coleslaws ⚓⚓⚓⚓⚓⚓⚓⚓

Many of us probably think of coleslaw as a typically American food. A favorite at picnics, barbecues and at the diner, it's a perfect side dish for burgers, hot dogs and sandwiches. Feel free to prepare the cabbage however you prefer when making coleslaw. Whether sliced paper thin, shredded or chopped, by hand or by food processor, you'll find the results delicious. In order to ensure that the cabbage remains crisp, presoak it in ice water and thoroughly drain before mixing it with the dressing. One pound of red or green cabbage will yield about 6 cups of shredded cabbage.

Old-fashioned Coleslaw

Coleslaw is not an American invention. It is thought to have been brought to this country by either German or Dutch immigrants. The Dutch called their salad *koolsla* (cabbage salad). And the word "cole" is the old English translation of the German word *kohl*, which means "cabbage." We do know that the first coleslaws were made using a boiled dressing. Sweet-and-sour and rich with sour cream, our Old-fashioned Coleslaw recipe boasts a traditional New England flavor.

3 tablespoons sugar

2 tablespoons all-purpose flour

1 teaspoon dry mustard

¹/₂ teaspoon salt

¹/₈ teaspoon ground red pepper (cayenne)

1 egg

³/₄ cup water

¹/₄ cup lemon juice

1 tablespoon margarine or butter

¹/₄ cup sour cream

1 pound green cabbage, shredded or finely chopped (about 6 cups)

1 medium carrot, shredded (about 1 cup)

1 small bell pepper, finely chopped (about ¹/₂ cup)

Mix sugar, flour, mustard, salt and red pepper in heavy 1-quart saucepan; beat in egg. Stir in water and lemon juice gradually until well blended. Cook over low heat 13 to 15 minutes, stirring constantly, until thick and smooth; remove from heat. Stir in margarine until melted. Place plastic wrap directly on surface of dressing; refrigerate about 2 hours or until cool. Stir in sour cream.

Mix dressing, cabbage, carrot and bell pepper; toss well. Refrigerate at least 1 hour but no longer than 24 hours. *8 servings.*

APPLE-CHEESE COLESLAW: Omit carrot and bell pepper; stir in 1 tart apple, chopped, and ¹/₄ cup crumbled blue cheese.

Nutrition Information Per Serving

1 serving

Calories	90	Fat, g	4
Protein, g	2	Cholesterol, mg	35
Carbohydrate, g	11	Sodium, mg	170

Sweet-Sour Coleslaw

Personal taste and ethnic background have been important factors in the great diversity of coleslaw recipes. The Pennsylvania Dutch, originally from southern Germany, added a boiled dressing that they used on both coleslaw and potato salad. The secret to their classic boiled dressing was to cook the dressing quickly and not let the eggs clump. For the best flavor, this Sweet-Sour Coleslaw should be covered and refrigerated for 2 to 4 hours before serving.

1 egg

¼ cup sugar

¼ cup vinegar

2 tablespoons water

2 tablespoons margarine or butter

1 teaspoon salt

½ teaspoon dry mustard

1 pound green cabbage, finely shredded or chopped (about 4 cups)

1 small bell pepper, chopped (about ½ cup)

Beat egg until thick and lemon colored. Heat sugar, vinegar, water, margarine, salt and mustard to boiling, stirring constantly. Gradually stir at least half of the hot mixture into egg; then stir into hot mixture in saucepan. Cook over low heat, stirring constantly, until thickened, about 5 minutes. Pour over cabbage and bell pepper; toss. *6 servings*.

Nutrition Information Per Serving

1 serving

Calories	105	Fat, g	5
Protein, g	2	Cholesterol, mg	35
Carbohydrate, g	13	Sodium, mg	420

Coleslaw

We were well into the twentieth century before commercially produced, bottled mayonnaise became widely available. Many people turned to the convenience of mayonnaise to take the place of making their own boiled dressing. Plain, or combined with whipped cream or sour cream, mayonnaise was found to be a perfect topping for cabbage. Our mayonnaise and sour cream–based recipe for Coleslaw is creamy, crunchy and not too sweet—just the way Texans like it at their famous barbecues. The coleslaw keeps well for several days in the refrigerator; just keep it tightly covered.

½ cup sour cream or plain yogurt

¼ cup mayonnaise or salad dressing

1 teaspoon sugar

½ teaspoon dry mustard

½ teaspoon seasoned salt

⅛ teaspoon pepper

1 pound green cabbage, finely shredded or chopped (about 4 cups)

1 small onion, chopped (about ¼ cup)

Paprika, if desired

Dill weed, if desired

Mix sour cream, mayonnaise, sugar, mustard, seasoned salt and pepper; toss with cabbage and onion. Sprinkle with paprika or dried dill weed, if desired. *8 servings*.

Nutrition Information Per Serving

1 serving

Calories	95	Fat, g	8
Protein, g	1	Cholesterol, mg	15
Carbohydrate, g	5	Sodium, mg	140

Farm-fried Potatoes

2 tablespoons shortening or vegetable oil

2 pounds potatoes (about 6 medium), thinly sliced (about 4 cups)

1 large onion, thinly sliced, if desired

1¹/₂ teaspoons salt

Dash of pepper

2 tablespoons margarine or butter

Heat shortening in 10-inch skillet until melted. Layer one-third of the potatoes and onion in skillet; sprinkle with ¹/₂ teaspoon of the salt and dash of pepper. Repeat 2 times. Dot with margarine. Cover and cook over medium heat 20 minutes. Uncover and cook, turning once, until potatoes are brown. *4 servings.*

Nutrition Information Per Serving

1 serving			
Calories	230	Fat, g	12
Protein, g	2	Cholesterol, mg	0
Carbohydrate, g	28	Sodium, mg	870

Candied Sweet Potatoes

6 medium sweet potatoes or yams (about 2 pounds)*

¹/₂ cup packed brown sugar

3 tablespoons margarine or butter

3 tablespoons water

¹/₂ teaspoon salt

Heat enough water (salted if desired) to cover potatoes to boiling. Add potatoes. Cover and heat to boiling; reduce heat. Boil until tender, 30 to 35 minutes. Drain and cool slightly. Slip off skins. Cut potatoes into ¹/₂-inch slices.

Heat remaining ingredients in 8-inch skillet over medium heat, stirring constantly, until smooth and bubbly. Add potato slices; stir gently until glazed and hot. *4 servings.*

BRANDY SWEET POTATOES: Substitute brandy for the water.

ORANGE SWEET POTATOES: Substitute orange juice for the water and add 1 tablespoon grated orange peel.

PINEAPPLE SWEET POTATOES: Omit water; add 1 can (8¹/₄ ounces) crushed pineapple in syrup, undrained.

SPICY SWEET POTATOES: Stir ¹/₂ teaspoon ground cinnamon or ¹/₄ teaspoon ground allspice, cloves, mace or nutmeg into brown sugar mixture in skillet.

Nutrition Information Per Serving

1 serving			
Calories	330	Fat, g	9
Protein, g	2	Cholesterol, mg	0
Carbohydrate, g	60	Sodium, mg	390

*1 can (23 ounces) sweet potatoes or yams, drained and cut into ¹/₂-inch slices, can be substituted for the sweet potatoes.

Hoppin' John

In South Carolina and neighboring states, it just wouldn't be a proper New Year's Day without a serving of Hoppin' John. This southern favorite is said to bring good luck for the coming year. Some believe Hoppin' John got its name because hungry children used to hop impatiently around the table as they waited for supper; others contend that it was named after the custom of inviting a guest to eat by saying "Hop in, John."

½ pound dried black-eyed peas (about 1 cup)

3½ cups water

¼ pound slab bacon, lean salt pork or smoked pork

1 onion, sliced

¼ to ½ teaspoon very finely chopped fresh hot chili or ⅛ to ¼ teaspoon crushed red pepper

½ cup uncooked regular long grain rice

1 teaspoon salt

Pepper

Heat peas and water to boiling in 2-quart saucepan; boil 2 minutes. Remove from heat; cover and let stand 1 hour. Cut bacon into 8 pieces. Stir bacon, onion and hot pepper into peas. Heat to boiling; reduce heat. Cover and simmer until peas are tender, 1 to 1½ hours.

Stir in rice, salt and pepper. Cover and simmer, stirring occasionally, until rice is tender, about 25 minutes. Stir in additional water, if necessary to cook rice. *6 servings*.

Nutrition Information Per Serving

1 serving

Calories	215	Fat, g	3
Protein, g	11	Cholesterol, mg	5
Carbohydrate, g	36	Sodium, mg	450

Fresh Tomato Salsa

2 medium tomatoes, finely chopped (about 1½ cups)

1 medium onion, chopped (about ½ cup)

1 small clove garlic, finely chopped

1 canned jalapeño chili, seeded and finely chopped

½ teaspoon jalapeño chili liquid (from jalapeño chili can)

1 tablespoon finely chopped cilantro, if desired

1 tablespoon lemon juice

1½ teaspoons vegetable oil

1½ teaspoons chopped fresh or ½ teaspoon dried oregano leaves

Mix all ingredients. Cover and refrigerate in glass or plastic container no longer than 7 days. *About 2 cups sauce*.

Nutrition Information Per Serving

1 tablespoon

Calories	5	Fat, g	0
Protein, g	0	Cholesterol, mg	0
Carbohydrate, g	1	Sodium, mg	15

Avocado-Citrus Salad

This unusual salad hails from the Southwest, but it could have easily come from Florida. Both regions have the ideal climate and the light, sandy soil that are perfect for growing oranges, grapefruits and avocados. Look for avocados that are ripe but still somewhat firm to the touch, yielding to gentle pressure. You'll love the fresh and delicious combination of rich, creamy avocado; tart grapefruit; and tangy orange.

2 tablespoons lime juice
2 tablespoons olive oil
1 tablespoon chopped fresh mint leaves
Lettuce
2 small avocados, sliced
1 grapefruit, pared and sliced
1 large orange, pared and sliced
¹/₄ cup chopped red onion

Mix lime juice, olive oil and mint; reserve. Line 4 salad plates with lettuce. Arrange avocado, grapefruit and orange slices on lettuce. Sprinkle with red onion. Drizzle with reserved lime juice mixture. *4 servings.*

Nutrition Information Per Serving

1 serving			
Calories	270	Fat, g	20
Protein, g	3	Cholesterol, mg	0
Carbohydrate, g	19	Sodium, mg	10

Iowa Peas and Cheese Salad

¹/₃ to ¹/₂ cup mayonnaise or salad dressing
¹/₂ teaspoon salt
¹/₂ teaspoon prepared mustard
¹/₄ teaspoon sugar
¹/₈ teaspoon pepper
2 cups cooked shelled fresh green peas*
1 cup diced mild Cheddar or Colby cheese
1 medium stalk celery, thinly sliced (about ¹/₂ cup)
3 sweet pickles, chopped (about ¹/₄ cup)
2 tablespoons finely chopped onion
2 hard-cooked eggs, chopped

Mix mayonnaise, salt, mustard, sugar and pepper in 2¹/₂-quart bowl. Add peas, cheese, celery, pickles and onion; toss. Stir in eggs. Cover and refrigerate until chilled, at least 1 hour. Serve on lettuce leaves, if desired. Immediately refrigerate any remaining salad. *6 servings.*

KIDNEY BEAN AND CHEESE SALAD: Substitute 1 can (15 ounces) kidney beans, rinsed and drained, for the fresh green peas.

Nutrition Information Per Serving

1 serving			
Calories	240	Fat, g	18
Protein, g	9	Cholesterol, mg	100
Carbohydrate, g	10	Sodium, mg	500

*1 package (10 ounces) frozen green peas, thawed and drained, can be substituted for the fresh green peas.

Avocado-Citrus Salad

Country Potato Salad

6 medium potatoes (about 2 pounds)

¹/₄ cup Italian dressing

Cooked Salad Dressing (below) or 1 cup mayonnaise or salad dressing

2 medium stalks celery, sliced (about 1 cup)

1 medium cucumber, chopped (about 1 cup)

1 large onion, chopped (about ³/₄ cup)

6 radishes, thinly sliced (about ¹/₂ cup)

4 hard-cooked eggs, chopped

Heat 1 inch water (salted if desired) to boiling. Add potatoes. Cover and heat to boiling; reduce heat. Cook until tender, 30 to 35 minutes. Drain and cool slightly. Peel potatoes; cut into cubes (about 6 cups). Toss warm potatoes with Italian dressing in 4-quart glass or plastic bowl. Cover and refrigerate at least 4 hours. Prepare Cooked Salad Dressing.

Add celery, cucumber, onion, radishes and eggs to potatoes. Pour Cooked Salad Dressing over top; toss. Refrigerate until chilled. Immediately refrigerate any remaining salad. *10 servings.*

COOKED SALAD DRESSING

2 tablespoons all-purpose flour
1 tablespoon sugar
1 teaspoon dry mustard
³/₄ teaspoon salt
¹/₄ teaspoon pepper
1 egg yolk, slightly beaten
³/₄ cup milk
2 tablespoons vinegar
1 tablespoon margarine or butter

Mix flour, sugar, mustard, salt and pepper in 1-quart saucepan. Mix egg yolk and milk; slowly stir into flour mixture. Cook over medium heat, stirring constantly, until mixture thickens and boils. Boil and stir 1 minute; remove from heat. Stir in vinegar and margarine. Place plastic wrap directly on surface; refrigerate until cool, at least 1 hour.

Nutrition Information Per Serving

1 serving			
Calories	165	Fat, g	7
Protein, g	5	Cholesterol, mg	110
Carbohydrate, g	21	Sodium, mg	270

Cranberry Salad Mold

³/₄ cup boiling water

1 package (3 ounces) raspberry-flavored gelatin

¹/₂ cup coarsely chopped nuts

¹/₃ cup chopped celery

1 can (16 ounces) whole berry cranberry sauce

1 can (8¹/₄ ounces) crushed pineapple in syrup, undrained

Pour boiling water on gelatin in 2-quart bowl; stir until gelatin is dissolved. Stir in remaining ingredients. Pour mixture into 5-cup mold. Refrigerate until firm; unmold. Garnish with salad greens, if desired. *8 servings.*

Nutrition Information Per Serving

1 serving			
Calories	165	Fat, g	5
Protein, g	1	Cholesterol, mg	0
Carbohydrate, g	29	Sodium, mg	25

Country Potato Salad, Heartland Three-Bean Salad (page 64)

Hot German Potato Salad

4 medium potatoes (about 1¹/₂ pounds)

3 slices bacon

1 medium onion, chopped (about ¹/₂ cup)

1 tablespoon all-purpose flour

1 tablespoon sugar

1 teaspoon salt

¹/₄ teaspoon celery seed

Dash of pepper

¹/₂ cup water

¹/₄ cup vinegar

Heat 1 inch water (salted if desired) to boiling. Add potatoes. Cover and heat to boiling; reduce heat. Cook until tender, 30 to 35 minutes; drain.

Cook bacon in 8-inch skillet until crisp; remove bacon and drain. Cook and stir onion in bacon fat until tender. Stir in flour, sugar, salt, celery seed and pepper. Cook over low heat, stirring constantly, until bubbly; remove from heat. Stir in water and vinegar. Heat to boiling, stirring constantly. Boil and stir 1 minute; remove from heat. Crumble bacon into hot mixture, then slice in warm potatoes. Cook, stirring gently to coat potato slices, until hot and bubbly. *5 servings.*

Nutrition Information Per Serving

1 serving

Calories	140	Fat, g	2
Protein, g	3	Cholesterol, mg	5
Carbohydrate, g	28	Sodium, mg	490

Heartland Three-Bean Salad

Three-bean salads are picnic favorites in the heartland. But not everyone agrees on which three beans to include in this hearty salad. You can count on finding green beans and wax beans in most recipes; and while many recipes—including ours—use kidney beans, there are some that call for lima beans instead. Of course, you can add lima beans to this recipe and enjoy a four-bean salad!

1 can (16 ounces) cut green beans, drained

1 can (16 ounces) cut wax beans, drained

1 can (15 ounces) kidney beans, drained

1 cup thinly sliced onion rings, cut in half

1 small bell pepper, finely chopped (about ¹/₂ cup)

2 tablespoons chopped fresh parsley

²/₃ cup vinegar

¹/₂ cup sugar

¹/₃ cup vegetable oil

¹/₂ teaspoon pepper

¹/₂ teaspoon salt

2 slices bacon, crisply cooked and crumbled

Mix beans, onion, bell pepper and parsley in 3-quart bowl. Mix remaining ingredients in 1¹/₂-quart saucepan. Heat vinegar mixture to boiling, stirring occasionally. Pour over beans; stir. Cover and refrigerate, stirring occasionally, at least 3 hours or until chilled. Just before serving, sprinkle with bacon. *12 servings.*

Nutrition Information Per Serving

1 serving
Calories	165	Fat, g	7
Protein, g	4	Cholesterol, mg	0
Carbohydrate, g	21	Sodium, mg	380

Wilted Spinach Salad

*1 medium onion, chopped (about ¹/₂
cup)*

1 slice bacon, cut up

1 clove garlic, finely chopped

2 tablespoons margarine or butter

2 tablespoons olive or vegetable oil

¹/₂ teaspoon salt

¹/₄ teaspoon pepper

¹/₄ teaspoon ground nutmeg

1 pound spinach

Juice of ¹/₂ lemon (about 2 tablespoons)

Cook and stir onion, bacon and garlic in margarine and oil in Dutch oven over medium heat until bacon is crisp; reduce heat. Stir in salt, pepper and nutmeg. Add spinach; toss just until spinach is wilted. Drizzle with lemon juice. *6 servings.*

Nutrition Information Per Serving

1 serving
Calories	105	Fat, g	9
Protein, g	2	Cholesterol, mg	0
Carbohydrate, g	4	Sodium, mg	280

Perfection Salad

A Pennsylvania woman won a sewing machine for this recipe entered in a cooking contest in the early years of the twentieth century. Popular at farm gatherings, it's easy to make ahead and adds pretty color and a cool, refreshing flavor to a robust country meal. By the 1930s, electric refrigerators and sweetened flavored gelatins inspired the creation of many new gelatin salads.

1 cup boiling water

*1 package (3 ounces) lemon-flavored
gelatin*

1 cup cold water

2 tablespoons lemon juice or vinegar

1 teaspoon salt

1 cup finely diced celery

1 cup finely shredded green cabbage

¹/₃ cup chopped sweet pickles

2 tablespoons finely chopped pimientos

Pour boiling water on gelatin in 2-quart bowl; stir until gelatin is dissolved. Stir in cold water, lemon juice and salt. Refrigerate until slightly thickened but not set. Stir in remaining ingredients. Pour into 4-cup mold or 6 individual molds. Refrigerate until firm; unmold. *6 servings.*

Nutrition Information Per Serving

1 serving
Calories	30	Fat, g	0
Protein, g	1	Cholesterol, mg	0
Carbohydrate, g	7	Sodium, mg	470

4

Warm from the Oven

Baked goods are a cherished part of any meal, whether breakfast, lunch or dinner. They are greatly appreciated between meals as well! Early settlers, far from stores and bakeries, learned to bake their own bread, muffins, coffee cakes, biscuits and other staples.

As with other foods, regional items were incorporated into recipes that settlers had brought from home, while other recipes were created from the foods at hand. Juicy blueberries were added to muffins, southerners perfected their biscuits and created Hush Puppies from cornmeal, and Jewish immigrants incorporated the newly marketed baking powder to streamline their rich Sour Cream Coffee Cake.

Corn has been a major crop since the first Europeans came to America. Native Americans taught the settlers how to grow corn, and make Shawnee cakes or pones, the forerunner of corn bread. This popular bread, quick and easy to make, has been served on country tables in many delicious ways and we have gathered the most luscious variations here for you to choose the one that best fits your mood and your meal.

Blueberry Muffins (page 68) and Baked Apple Butter (page 86)

67

Blueberry Muffins

Colonists in New England initially confused the blueberry with a common English berry, the bilberry. From country kitchens to city coffee shops, the all-American blueberry muffin is one of our very favorite morning treats. You can find blueberries growing from North Carolina on up to Alaska. This tried-and-true New England recipe makes some of the best blueberry muffins you'll ever taste!

1 egg

³/₄ cup milk

1 cup fresh or ³/₄ cup frozen (thawed and well drained) blueberries

¹/₃ cup vegetable oil

¹/₄ cup honey

2 cups all-purpose or whole wheat flour

3 teaspoons baking powder

¹/₂ teaspoon salt

¹/₄ cup packed brown sugar

¹/₂ teaspoon ground cinnamon

Heat oven to 400°. Grease bottoms only of about 12 medium muffin cups, 2¹/₂ × 1¹/₄ inches, or line with paper baking cups. Beat egg in 2¹/₂-quart bowl; stir in milk, blueberries, oil and honey. Stir in remaining ingredients all at once just until flour is moistened (batter will be lumpy). Divide batter evenly among muffin cups (about three-fourths full). Mix brown sugar and cinnamon; sprinkle over batter. Bake until golden brown, about 20 minutes. Immediately remove from pan. *About 12 muffins.*

HONEY-BRAN MUFFINS: Increase milk to 1¹/₂ cups. Pour milk over 1¹/₂ cups whole wheat bran cereal; let stand 2 minutes. Stir in with the oil. Sprinkle with brown sugar-cinnamon mixture, if desired.

HONEY-NUT MUFFINS: Substitute ¹/₂ cup chopped nuts for the blueberries. Sprinkle with brown sugar-cinnamon mixture, if desired.

Nutrition Information Per Serving

1 muffin

Calories	200	Fat, g	10
Protein, g	3	Cholesterol, mg	20
Carbohydrate, g	25	Sodium, mg	200

Mountain Bran Muffins

Mornings start early on farms, so fresh muffins from a homemade mix can be a real boon to hardworking families. This handy mix—based on a cherished bran bread recipe from the Colorado mountains—can be stored in a cool, dry place. When you don't have much time, and you're longing for a rich, moist bran muffin packed with walnuts and raisins, you'll be all ready to go!

1 cup buttermilk

1 egg

2¹/₂ cups Mountain Bran Mix (right)

¹/₂ cup chopped walnuts

¹/₂ cup raisins

Heat oven to 400°. Grease bottoms only of 12 medium muffin cups, 2¹/₂ × 1¹/₄ inches, or line with paper baking cups. Beat buttermilk and egg in large bowl. Stir in Mountain Bran Mix just until moistened; fold in walnuts and raisins. Divide batter evenly among muffin cups (about seven-eighths full). Bake until golden brown or toothpick inserted in center comes out clean, 18 to 20 minutes. Let stand 3 minutes; remove muffins from pan. *12 muffins.*

MOUNTAIN BRAN MIX

3 cups all-purpose flour
3 cups Fiber One® cereal, finely crushed
2 cups packed brown sugar
1¹/₂ teaspoons baking soda
1¹/₂ teaspoons baking powder
1¹/₂ teaspoons salt
¹/₂ cup shortening

Mix flour, cereal, brown sugar, baking soda, baking powder and salt in 4-quart bowl. Cut in shortening until mixture resembles coarse crumbs. Cover and store in cool, dry place no longer than 1 month. *About 7¹/₂ cups mix (enough for 3 dozen muffins).*

Nutrition Information Per Serving

1 muffin

Calories	200	Fat, g	7
Protein, g	3	Cholesterol, mg	20
Carbohydrate, g	31	Sodium, mg	200

Dixie Biscuits

The South is famous for its biscuits—and with good reason. Beaten biscuits, buttermilk biscuits and these wonderfully light and flaky baking powder biscuits are all Dixieland favorites. They used to appear on the table for each and every meal in the South. To ensure tender, flaky biscuits, knead the dough very lightly. When cutting the dough, try not to twist the cutter; press down and pull straight up. Southern biscuits, by tradition, are pricked with a fork to make them thinner.

1³/₄ cups all-purpose flour or 2 cups cake flour
2¹/₂ teaspoons baking powder
³/₄ teaspoon salt*
¹/₃ cup shortening or firm margarine or butter
³/₄ cup milk

Mix flour, baking powder and salt. Cut in shortening until mixture resembles fine crumbs. Stir in almost all the milk. Stir in just enough additional milk to make a soft, puffy, easy-to-roll dough. (Too much milk makes dough sticky; not enough makes biscuits dry.)

Heat oven to 425°. Shape dough into ball on lightly floured cloth-covered surface. (If using all-purpose flour, knead about 10 times.) Pat into circle about ¹/₂ inch thick with floured hands. Fold into thirds; pat again into circle about ¹/₂ inch thick. Cut with floured 1³/₄-inch biscuit cutter.

Place on ungreased cookie sheet 1 inch apart for crusty sides, close together for soft sides. Prick each biscuit several times with fork. Brush with slightly beaten egg or evaporated milk, if desired. Bake until golden brown, 12 to 15 minutes. Serve hot. *About 16 biscuits.*

Nutrition Information Per Serving

1 biscuit

Calories	95	Fat, g	5
Protein, g	2	Cholesterol, mg	0
Carbohydrate, g	11	Sodium, mg	170

*If using salted margarine or butter, decrease salt to ¹/₂ teaspoon.

Hush Puppies

Vegetable oil

1½ cups cornmeal

½ cup all-purpose flour

¼ cup shortening

1 cup milk

2 tablespoons finely chopped onion

2 teaspoons baking powder

1 teaspoon sugar

1 teaspoon salt

½ teaspoon baking soda

¼ to ½ teaspoon ground red pepper (cayenne)

1 egg

Heat oil (1 inch) in Dutch oven to 375°. Mix remaining ingredients. Drop by teaspoonfuls into hot oil. Fry, turning once, until golden brown, about 1 minute; drain. *About 4 dozen hush puppies.*

Nutrition Information Per Serving

1 hush puppy

Calories	80	Fat, g	6
Protein, g	1	Cholesterol, mg	5
Carbohydrate, g	5	Sodium, mg	75

Popovers

Warm, crusty popovers will delight children and adults alike. Southerners are particularly fond of them, but everyone loves the surprise of breaking into one of these puffy, golden brown treats and finding just air inside! Even though it's very tempting, resist peeking in the oven during the first 20-minute baking period because a change in heat will cause the wonderful balloonlike shape to collapse.

2 eggs

1 cup all-purpose flour

1 cup milk

½ teaspoon salt

Heat oven to 450°. Generously grease 6-cup popover pan or six 6-ounce custard cups. Beat eggs slightly; beat in remaining ingredients just until smooth (do not overbeat). Fill custard cups about one-half full. Bake 20 minutes. Reduce oven temperature to 350°; bake 20 minutes longer. Immediately remove from cups; serve hot. *6 popovers.*

Nutrition Information Per Serving

1 popover

Calories	120	Fat, g	3
Protein, g	5	Cholesterol, mg	75
Carbohydrate, g	18	Sodium, mg	220

Popovers with Strawberry-Rhubarb Jam (page 85)

Praline Bread

Pralines, pecans suspended in a rich golden brown sugar mixture, are a New Orleans specialty. Native to the Mississippi valley, pecans show up all over southern cooking. You will also find the same wonderful praline flavor in Praline Sweet Potato Pie (page 104) and Apple-Praline Pie (page 107).

2 cups all-purpose or unbleached flour

1 teaspoon baking powder

1/2 teaspoon salt

1/2 cup (1 stick) margarine or butter, softened

1/2 cup granulated sugar

1/2 cup packed brown sugar

1 teaspoon vanilla

1/2 teaspoon maple extract

2 eggs

3/4 cup milk

1 cup chopped pecans, toasted

Heat oven to 350°. Grease bottom only of loaf pan, 8½ × 4½ × 2½ or 9 × 5 × 3 inches. Mix flour, baking powder and salt; reserve. Beat margarine and the sugars in 3-quart bowl on medium speed until light and fluffy. Beat in vanilla, maple extract and 1 egg. Beat in remaining egg. Beat in reserved flour mixture alternately with milk on low speed, beating well after each addition. Reserve 2 tablespoons pecans. Mix remaining pecans into batter; pour into pan. Finely chop reserved pecans; sprinkle over batter. Bake until toothpick inserted in center comes out clean, 55 to 65 minutes. Cool 10 minutes; remove from pan. Cool completely before slicing. *1 loaf (about 24 slices).*

Praline Bread, Sticky Buns (page 80)

Nutrition Information Per Serving

1 slice

Calories	150	Fat, g	8
Protein, g	2	Cholesterol, mg	20
Carbohydrate, g	18	Sodium, mg	115

Brown Bread

1/2 cup all-purpose or rye flour

1/2 cup cornmeal

1/2 cup whole wheat flour

1/2 cup currants or chopped raisins

1 cup buttermilk

1/3 cup molasses

1 teaspoon baking soda

1 teaspoon grated orange peel

1/2 teaspoon salt

Grease loaf pan, 8½ × 4½ × 2½ inches. Beat all ingredients in 3-quart bowl on low speed, scraping bowl constantly, 30 seconds. Beat on medium speed, scraping bowl constantly, 30 seconds longer. Pour into pan. Cover tightly with aluminum foil.

Place pan on rack in Dutch oven or steamer; pour boiling water into pan to level of rack. Cover Dutch oven. Keep water boiling over low heat until toothpick inserted in center comes out clean, about 2½ hours. (Add boiling water during steaming if necessary.) Remove pan from Dutch oven; immediately remove bread from pan. Serve warm. *1 loaf (24 slices).*

Nutrition Information Per Serving

1 slice

Calories	50	Fat, g	0
Protein, g	1	Cholesterol, mg	0
Carbohydrate, g	12	Sodium, mg	90

Country Corn Breads ✶✶✶✶✶✶✶

Corn bread is one of America's favorite quick breads. Easy and quick to make, it's a hearty way to satisfy a longing for warm-from-the-oven homemade bread. Delicious when hot, corn bread is also wonderful when cooled, sliced and thickly spread with butter or jam, or when toasted the next day.

Traditional Corn Bread

Corn has been among our most important crops from colonial days right up until today. It was unfamiliar to the first colonists because it is native to the Americas, and had never been seen in Europe. But the colonists followed the example of Native Americans and made fried corn bread, called Shawnee cakes or pones, over an open fire. Later, a mixture of cornmeal, salt and water baked on the flat side of a cotton hoe became known as hoe cakes. Skillet corn bread became known as journey bread (because it traveled well) or "Johnnycakes." Rhode Islanders put their own stamp on them by dropping the "h" and using white rather than yellow cornmeal. The corn bread we enjoy most often today has changed with the additions of flour, baking soda and baking powder. These new, lighter breads, sometimes made with buttermilk, have become a favorite in the Northeast and throughout the country.

1¹/₂ cups yellow cornmeal

¹/₂ cup all-purpose flour

¹/₄ cup shortening or bacon fat

1¹/₂ cups buttermilk

2 teaspoons baking powder

1 teaspoon sugar

1 teaspoon salt

¹/₂ teaspoon baking soda

2 eggs

Heat oven to 450°. Grease round pan, 9 × 1¹/₂ inches, or square pan, 8 × 8 × 2 inches. Mix all ingredients; beat vigorously 30 seconds. Pour batter into pan. Bake until golden brown, 25 to 30 minutes. Serve warm. *12 servings.*

CORN STICKS: Fill 18 greased corn stick pans about seven-eighths full. Bake 12 to 15 minutes.

SKILLET CORN BREAD: Pour batter into greased 10-inch ovenproof skillet. Bake about 20 minutes.

Nutrition Information Per Serving

1 serving

Calories	145	Fat, g	6
Protein, g	4	Cholesterol, mg	35
Carbohydrate, g	19	Sodium, mg	320

Sweet Corn Bread Muffins

Midwesterners like their corn bread richer and sweeter than in other regions. Cornmeal is available in textures ranging from fine to coarse. Grocery stores commonly carry a finely ground cornmeal which will make a light, soft bread. The coarser cornmeals, often called stone ground, give breads a stronger flavor and coarser texture. Stone-ground cornmeal is delicious in this recipe.

1 cup milk

¼ cup (½ stick) margarine or butter, melted

1 egg

1¼ cups cornmeal

1 cup all-purpose flour

½ cup sugar

1 tablespoon baking powder

½ teaspoon salt

Heat oven to 400°. Grease bottoms only of 12 medium muffin cups, 2½ × 1¼ inches, or line with paper baking cups. Beat milk, margarine and egg in 3-quart bowl. Stir in remaining ingredients all at once just until flour is moistened (batter will be lumpy). Fill muffin cups about three-fourths full. Bake until golden brown and toothpick inserted in center comes out clean, 20 to 25 minutes. *12 muffins.*

SWEET CORN BREAD: Pour batter into greased round pan, 9 × 1½ inches, or square pan, 8 × 8 × 2 inches. Bake as directed.

Nutrition Information Per Serving

1 muffin

Calories	170	Fat, g	5
Protein, g	3	Cholesterol, mg	20
Carbohydrate, g	28	Sodium, mg	240

Chili-Cheese Corn Bread

Every encounter with corn bread in the Southwest is bound to be interesting. It's rare to see a plain corn bread there. Cooks often stir in green chilies, sweet corn or cheese. Our Chili-Cheese Corn Bread is full of delicious Tex-Mex flavor. Serve this zesty corn bread with all of your southwestern favorites—it's especially good with a big bowl of hot chili!

1 cup all-purpose flour

1 cup yellow cornmeal

1 cup shredded Cheddar cheese (4 ounces)

1 cup cooked fresh whole kernel corn*

¼ cup shortening

1 cup milk

2 tablespoons sugar

4 teaspoons baking powder

½ teaspoon salt

1 can (4 ounces) chopped green chilies, drained

1 egg

Heat oven to 425°. Grease square pan, 9 × 9 × 2 inches. Mix all ingredients until moistened. Beat vigorously 30 seconds. Pour into pan. Bake until golden brown, 20 to 25 minutes. *9 servings.*

Nutrition Information Per Serving

1 serving

Calories	270	Fat, g	12
Protein, g	8	Cholesterol, mg	40
Carbohydrate, g	32	Sodium, mg	610

* 1 can (7 ounces) whole kernel corn, drained, or 1 cup frozen whole kernel corn, thawed and drained, can be substituted for fresh corn.

Pull-apart Bread

Bread is just about the most important food staple there is. Cooks in the West varied their bread by cutting the dough into pieces, dipping each piece in butter, and baking them all together in a deep pan. The delightful pull-apart loaf that results from this unusual technique is usually called monkey bread or bubble loaf. For fun variations, after rolling the balls in butter, roll them in a cinnamon and sugar mixture or in a savory blend of fragrant herbs.

3¹/₂ to 3³/₄ cups all-purpose flour

2 tablespoons sugar

¹/₂ teaspoon salt

1 package quick-acting active dry yeast

1 cup milk

¹/₄ cup (¹/₂ stick) margarine or butter

1 egg

¹/₄ cup (¹/₂ stick) margarine or butter, melted

Grease 12-cup bundt cake pan or tube pan, 10 × 4 inches. Mix 1¹/₂ cups of the flour, the sugar, salt and yeast in 3-quart bowl. Heat milk and ¹/₄ cup margarine in 1-quart saucepan over medium-low heat, stirring frequently, until very warm (120° to 130°). Add milk mixture and egg to flour mixture. Beat on low speed until moistened; beat 3 minutes on medium speed. Stir in enough remaining flour to make dough easy to handle.

Turn dough onto lightly floured surface. Knead until smooth and elastic, about 5 minutes. Shape dough into 24 balls. Dip each ball of dough into the melted margarine. Layer evenly in pan. Cover and let rise in warm place until double, 20 to 30 minutes.

Heat oven to 350°. Bake until golden brown, 25 to 30 minutes. Cool 2 minutes; invert onto heatproof serving plate. Serve warm. *1 loaf (12 servings).*

Nutrition Information Per Serving

1 serving

Calories	225	Fat, g	9
Protein, g	5	Cholesterol, mg	20
Carbohydrate, g	31	Sodium, mg	190

Pull-apart Bread and Raisin Oatmeal Bread (page 79)

Sour Cream Coffee Cake

Baking powder, which became commercially available in the 1860s and was widely used by the 1880s, inspired many new cake recipes. Jewish immigrants used it to speed preparation of this rich and hearty coffee cake. Layered with a delicious nut filling and drizzled with a pretty powdered sugar glaze, it's an easy and popular cake to serve at morning get-togethers.

Cinnamon Filling or Almond Filling (below)

1¹/₂ cups sugar

³/₄ cup (1¹/₂ sticks) margarine or butter, softened

1¹/₂ teaspoons vanilla

3 eggs

3 cups all-purpose or whole wheat flour

1¹/₂ teaspoons baking powder

1¹/₂ teaspoons baking soda

³/₄ teaspoon salt

1¹/₂ cups sour cream

¹/₂ cup powdered sugar

¹/₄ teaspoon vanilla

1 to 2 teaspoons milk

Heat oven to 325°. Grease tube pan, 10 × 4 inches, or 12-cup bundt cake pan. Prepare Cinnamon Filling; reserve. Beat sugar, margarine, vanilla and eggs in 2¹/₂-quart bowl on medium speed, scraping bowl occasionally, 2 minutes. Beat in flour, baking powder, baking soda and salt alternately with sour cream on low speed. Spread one-third of the batter (about 2 cups) in pan; sprinkle with one-third of the filling (about ¹/₃ cup). Repeat 2 times. Bake until toothpick inserted near center comes out clean, about 1 hour. Cool 20 minutes; remove from pan. Mix remaining ingredients until smooth and of de-sired consistency; drizzle over coffee cake. *16 servings.*

CINNAMON FILLING

¹/₂ cup packed brown sugar
¹/₂ cup finely chopped nuts
1¹/₂ teaspoons ground cinnamon

Mix all ingredients.

ALMOND FILLING

¹/₂ package (7- to 8.8-ounce size) almond paste, cut into small pieces
¹/₂ cup powdered sugar
¹/₄ cup (¹/₂ stick) margarine or butter
¹/₂ cup sliced almonds

Cook almond paste, powdered sugar and margarine over medium heat, stirring constantly, until smooth; stir in almonds.

Nutrition Information Per Serving

1 serving			
Calories	355	Fat, g	16
Protein, g	4	Cholesterol, mg	55
Carbohydrate, g	49	Sodium, mg	340

Garden Wheat Batter Bread

2 cups whole wheat flour

1 package quick-acting active dry yeast

1 teaspoon salt

1¼ cups water

2 tablespoons honey

2 tablespoons margarine or butter

1 cup all-purpose or unbleached flour

1 small carrot, finely shredded (about ¼ cup)

1 tablespoon chopped fresh parsley

Mix whole wheat flour, yeast and salt in 3-quart bowl. Heat water, honey and margarine in 1-quart saucepan over medium-low heat until very warm (120° to 130°). Add to wheat flour mixture; beat on low speed until moistened, scraping bowl occasionally. Beat 3 minutes on medium speed. (By hand, beat 300 vigorous strokes.) Stir in all-purpose flour, carrot and parsley. Scrape batter from side of bowl. Cover and let rise in warm place until double, about 20 minutes.

Generously grease loaf pan, 8½ × 4½ × 2½ or 9 × 5 × 3 inches. Stir down batter by beating about 25 strokes. Smooth and pat batter in loaf pan with floured hands. Cover and let rise in warm place until double, about 15 minutes.

Heat oven to 375°. Bake until loaf sounds hollow when tapped, 30 to 35 minutes. Immediately remove from pan. Brush top with melted margarine, if desired; cool on wire rack. *1 loaf (16 slices).*

Nutrition Information Per Serving

1 slice

Calories	105	Fat, g	2
Protein, g	3	Cholesterol, mg	0
Carbohydrate, g	19	Sodium, mg	150

Raisin-Oatmeal Bread

1½ cups water

1½ teaspoons salt

1½ cups quick-cooking oats

⅓ cup packed brown sugar

1 tablespoon shortening

1 package active dry yeast

¼ cup warm water (105° to 115°)

½ cup raisins

3 to 3¼ cups all-purpose flour

1 egg white, slightly beaten

2 tablespoons quick-cooking oats

Heat water and salt to boiling in 3-quart saucepan. Stir in 1½ cups oats, the brown sugar and shortening; cool to lukewarm. Dissolve yeast in ¼ cup warm water. Stir into oat mixture. Stir in raisins. Mix in flour with spoon (dough will be sticky). Turn dough onto lightly floured surface; knead until smooth and elastic, about 10 minutes. Place in greased bowl; turn greased side up. Cover; let rise in warm place (85°) until double, about 1½ hours. (If kitchen is cool, place dough on a rack over a bowl of hot water and cover completely with a towel.)

Grease loaf pan, 9 × 5 × 3 inches. Punch down dough; shape into rounded loaf. Place in pan. Brush top with egg white; sprinkle with 2 tablespoons oats. Cover; let rise in warm place until double, about 1 hour.

Heat oven to 375°. Bake until dark brown, 40 to 45 minutes. Remove from pan; cool on wire rack. *1 loaf (16 slices).*

Nutrition Information Per Serving

1 slice

Calories	160	Fat, g	2
Protein, g	4	Cholesterol, mg	0
Carbohydrate, g	32	Sodium, mg	210

Sticky Buns

With their nut-and-raisin filling and luscious glaze, sticky buns are an irresistible treat any time. Especially popular in Pennsylvania, they are a variation of *schnecken*, snail-shaped buns that are a specialty of the Pennsylvania Dutch.

1 package regular or quick-acting active dry yeast

½ cup warm water (105° to 115°)

½ cup lukewarm milk (scalded then cooled)

⅓ cup granulated sugar

⅓ cup shortening or margarine or butter, softened

1 teaspoon salt

1 egg

3½ to 4 cups all-purpose flour

1 cup packed brown sugar

½ cup (1 stick) margarine or butter

¼ cup corn syrup

2 tablespoons margarine or butter, softened

Pecan-Raisin Filling (below)

Dissolve yeast in warm water in 2½-quart bowl. Stir in milk, granulated sugar, shortening, salt, egg and 2 cups of the flour. Beat until smooth. Mix in enough remaining flour to make dough easy to handle. Turn dough onto lightly floured surface; knead until smooth and elastic, about 5 minutes.

Place in greased 2½-quart bowl; turn greased side up. Cover; let rise in warm place until double, about 1½ hours. (Dough is ready if indentation remains when touched.)

Heat brown sugar and ½ cup margarine to boiling in 1-quart saucepan, stirring constantly; re-move from heat. Stir in corn syrup; cool 5 minutes. Pour into greased rectangular pan, 13 × 9 × 2 inches.

Punch down dough. Flatten dough with hands or rolling pin into rectangle, 15 × 10 inches, on lightly floured surface; spread with 2 tablespoons margarine. Sprinkle Pecan-Raisin Filling evenly over margarine. Roll up tightly, beginning at 15-inch side. Pinch edge of dough into roll to seal well. Stretch roll to make even. Cut into fifteen 1-inch slices. Place slightly apart in pan. Let rise until double, about 40 minutes.

Heat oven to 375°. Bake until golden brown, 30 to 35 minutes. Immediately invert pan on heatproof tray. Let pan remain a minute so caramel can drizzle over rolls. Spoon any remaining caramel from tray over rolls. *15 rolls.*

PECAN-RAISIN FILLING

½ cup chopped pecans
½ cup raisins
1½ teaspoons ground cinnamon

Mix all ingredients.

Nutrition Information Per Serving

1 roll

Calories	360	Fat, g	16
Protein, g	4	Cholesterol, mg	15
Carbohydrate, g	50	Sodium, mg	250

Buckwheat Pancakes

1 egg
½ cup buckwheat flour
½ cup whole wheat flour
1 cup milk
1 tablespoon sugar
3 teaspoons baking powder
2 tablespoons shortening, melted, or vegetable oil
½ teaspoon salt
Whole bran or wheat germ, if desired

Beat egg with hand beater until fluffy; beat in remaining ingredients just until smooth. Grease heated griddle if necessary. (To test griddle, sprinkle with few drops water. If bubbles skitter around, heat is just right.)

For each pancake, pour about 3 tablespoons batter from tip of large spoon or from pitcher onto hot griddle. Cook pancakes until puffed and dry around edges. Sprinkle each pancake with 1 teaspoon whole bran. Turn and cook other sides until golden brown. *Ten 4-inch pancakes.*

BLUEBERRY PANCAKES: Substitute 1 cup all-purpose flour for the buckwheat and whole wheat flours. Decrease milk to ¾ cup. Stir in ½ cup fresh or frozen (thawed and well drained) blueberries.

Nutrition Information Per Serving

1 pancake

Calories	95	Fat, g	4
Protein, g	3	Cholesterol, mg	25
Carbohydrate, g	12	Sodium, mg	240

Nut Waffles

2 eggs
2 cups all-purpose or whole wheat flour
½ cup vegetable oil or margarine or butter, melted
1¾ cups milk
1 tablespoon granulated or brown sugar
4 teaspoons baking powder
¼ teaspoon salt
2 tablespoons coarsely chopped or broken nuts

Heat waffle iron. Beat eggs with hand beater in medium bowl until fluffy. Beat in remaining ingredients just until smooth. Pour batter from cup or pitcher onto center of hot waffle iron. Immediately sprinkle with nuts. Bake about 5 minutes or until steaming stops. Remove waffle carefully. *Twelve 4-inch waffle squares (three 9-inch waffles).*

Nutrition Information Per Serving

Calories	210	Fat, g	13
Protein, g	5	Cholesterol, mg	50
Carbohydrate, g	18	Sodium, mg	210

5

Putting Up the Harvest

The summer harvest is a major event, fresh fruits and vegetables tumbling ripe into boxes and baskets. And when you "put up" this bounty, you can have a taste of summer, no matter how cold and dreary the day!

In the country, canning, pickling and preserving was the way to keep the harvest on the kitchen shelves, long after summer had passed. Days were spent in canning kitchens, putting up the fruits and vegetables necessary to see a family through the winter. Today, with access to fruits and vegetables throughout the year, we "put up" the harvest to please our palate, not as a necessity.

You'll find these recipes have been streamlined for modern kitchens, letting you enjoy homemade Peach Preserves, Pumpkin Chutney, Watermelon Pickles and other treats whenever you wish. And with apples so plentiful and popular, we have included a regional round-up of apple butter recipes, sure to please everyone.

Peach Preserves (page 84)

Peach Preserves

Capturing the fresh taste of summer peaches on a wintry morning is a wonderful reason to make these preserves! If you need to ripen the peaches for the preserves, place them in a brown paper bag and close it securely. Check on their progress daily—ripe peaches will be soft, especially at the stem, and when pressed gently they have a lovely aroma. For maximum flavor, let the preserves mellow for a week before serving.

> *4 pounds peaches, peeled and sliced (about 8 cups)*
>
> *6 cups sugar*
>
> *¹/₄ cup lemon juice*

Toss peaches and sugar. Cover and refrigerate at least 12 hours but no longer than 24 hours.

Heat peach mixture to boiling, stirring constantly. Rapidly boil uncovered 20 minutes. Stir in lemon juice. Boil uncovered 10 minutes longer. Immediately pour mixture into hot sterilized jars, leaving ¹/₄-inch headspace. Wipe rims of jars. Seal and process in boiling water bath 15 minutes. *About 6 half-pints preserves.*

SPICED PEACH PRESERVES: Tie 8 whole cloves, 5 whole allspice, 2 sticks cinnamon, 2 blades mace and 1¹/₂ teaspoons ground coriander in cheesecloth bag; add to peach mixture before boiling. Remove spice bag before pouring mixture into jars.

Nutrition Information Per Serving

1 tablespoon

Calories	55	Fat, g	0
Protein, g	0	Cholesterol, mg	0
Carbohydrate, g	14	Sodium, mg	0

Mixed Berry Jam

Gone are the days when "putting by" jam was a summertime necessity to see one through the long winter months. Rather, we can now make jam when we find beautiful, ripe berries—and this jam is just right for showcasing juicy, fresh fruit. This uncooked jam, also called "freezer jam," became popular in the 1960s. You'll love it, too, when you realize just how easy and fast it is. Be sure to store this jam in the refrigerator or freezer.

> *1 cup crushed strawberries (about 1 pint whole berries)*
>
> *1 cup crushed raspberries (about 1 pint whole berries)*
>
> *4 cups sugar*
>
> *1 tablespoon lemon juice*
>
> *¹/₂ teaspoon grated lemon peel*
>
> *1 pouch (3 ounces) liquid fruit pectin*

Mix berries and sugar; let stand at room temperature, stirring occasionally, until sugar is dissolved, about 10 minutes. Mix in remaining ingredients; stir until slightly thickened, 3 to 5 minutes. Spoon mixture into freezer containers, leaving ¹/₂-inch headspace. Seal immediately. Let stand at room temperature 24 hours. Refrigerate no longer than 3 weeks or freeze no longer than 1 year. Thaw before serving. *About 5 half-pints jam.*

Nutrition Information Per Serving

1 tablespoon

Calories	40	Fat, g	0
Protein, g	0	Cholesterol, mg	0
Carbohydrate, g	10	Sodium, mg	0

Strawberry-Rhubarb Jam

How fortunate that strawberries and rhubarb are in season at the same time! The sharp tartness of rhubarb combines perfectly with the sweetness of plump red strawberries in this jam. Rhubarb, also known as "pie plant," is popular in American gardens, producing large stalks streaked with deep cherry red and green. You'll find that the deeper the red, the more beautiful the color of the jam, compote or pie. Be sure to use only the stalks of the rhubarb, because the leaves are poisonous.

> *3 cups crushed strawberries (about 1 quart whole berries)*
>
> *4 cups finely chopped rhubarb (about 1 pound)*
>
> *3 cups sugar*
>
> *1 stick cinnamon*

Mix all ingredients in Dutch oven; let stand 2 hours. Heat to boiling, stirring constantly, until mixture begins to thicken or reaches 220°, about 20 to 25 minutes. Remove from heat; quickly skim off foam. Remove cinnamon stick. Immediately pour mixture into hot sterilized jars, leaving ¼-inch headspace. Wipe rims of jars. Seal and process in boiling water bath 5 minutes. *About 4 half-pints jam.*

Nutrition Information Per Serving

1 tablespoon

Calories	40	Fat, g	0
Protein, g	0	Cholesterol, mg	0
Carbohydrate, g	10	Sodium, mg	0

Pumpkin Chutney

As the air becomes crisp and children's minds turn to trick-or-treating and jack-o'-lanterns, we celebrate the autumn harvest of such crops as apples, cranberries and pumpkins. In the past, thoughtful cooks preserved the glory of the fall pumpkin in chutneys they put up to last all winter. This sweet and spicy chutney, with its jamlike consistency, is wonderful served with roast turkey or in meat salads.

> *8 cups chopped pared pumpkin (about 6-pound pumpkin)*
>
> *4 cups packed brown sugar*
>
> *2 cups raisins*
>
> *1 cup chopped dates*
>
> *4 cups cider vinegar*
>
> *1 tablespoon mustard seed*
>
> *2 teaspoons salt*
>
> *2 teaspoons ground ginger*
>
> *2 teaspoons lemon peel*
>
> *2 teaspoons ground allspice*
>
> *1 large onion, chopped (about 1 cup)*
>
> *1 medium red bell pepper, chopped (about 1 cup)*

Heat all ingredients to boiling in 6-quart Dutch oven; reduce heat. Simmer uncovered, stirring frequently, until mixture thickens, 1½ to 1¾ hours. Immediately pour mixture into hot sterilized jars, leaving ½-inch headspace. Wipe rims of jars. Seal and process in boiling water bath 10 minutes. *About 6 pints chutney.*

Nutrition Information Per Serving

1 tablespoon

Calories	30	Fat, g	0
Protein, g	0	Cholesterol, mg	0
Carbohydrate, g	4	Sodium, mg	25

Delectable Apple Butters ❧❧❧❧❧❧

The Pilgrims brought with them a taste of the Old World when they carried apple trees to this country. We've all heard the story of "Johnny Appleseed," the man who roamed the country planting apple seeds. His real name was John Chapman, and in the early nineteenth century he traveled from the East Coast out to Ohio, Indiana and Illinois, bringing the settlers an important and reliable source of fruit.

Baked Apple Butter

Upstate New York is the home of baked apple butter. Farm women there came up with a way to do their chores, take care of children and make apple butter all at once. They didn't have the time to stir apple butter constantly, so they learned to bake it instead, which lets the oven do the work. Making traditional apple butter was often a messy and sticky event because as the apple mixture thickens, it spits and can spatter everything nearby. The oven method, on the other hand, results in a rich, brown butter without the problems of spattering, sticking or burning on the bottom of the pan. You'll find that this Baked Apple Butter is delicious slathered on roasted pork or, of course, on your morning toast.

24 cups pared, cored and quartered cooking apples (about 7 pounds)

2 cups apple cider or juice

1 cup cider vinegar

3 cups sugar

2 teaspoons ground cinnamon

1/2 teaspoon ground cloves

1/2 teaspoon ground allspice

Heat apples, apple cider and vinegar to boiling in 6-quart Dutch oven or stockpot; reduce heat. Simmer uncovered, stirring frequently, until apples are very soft, about 1 hour.

Heat oven to 350°. Press apple mixture through sieve or food mill, or mash with potato masher just until smooth. Stir in remaining ingredients. Pour mixture into stainless steel or enamel pan, 15¼ × 10½ × 2 inches.* Bake until no liquid separates from pulp, stirring every 30 minutes to prevent sticking, about 4 hours.

Immediately pour mixture into hot sterilized jars, leaving ¼-inch headspace. Wipe rims of jars. Seal and process in boiling water bath 10 minutes. *About 6 half-pints butter.*

Nutrition Information Per Serving

1 tablespoon

Calories	45	Fat, g	0
Protein, g	0	Cholesterol, mg	0
Carbohydrate, g	11	Sodium, mg	0

*A rectangular baking dish, 13 × 9 × 2 inches, can be used. Fill three-fourths full, adding remaining apple mixture as mixture in oven bakes down.

Apple Butter

The Pennsylvania Dutch, who are known for their skillful ways with preserves, use their abundant supply of apples to make one of their specialties, apple butter. In days gone by, making this spread called for a party. Many hands were needed to pare and slice the bushels of apples and to stir constantly the gallons of cooking apple butter to keep it from burning. These parties were called

"schnitzing parties" after the German word for slice, *schnitz*. (You may wonder why the Pennsylvania Dutch used a German word. The Pennsylvania Dutch were, in fact, German, but to American ears, *Deutsch*, which means German, sounded like "Dutch," and the misnomer stuck.)

4 quarts apple cider or juice

12 cups pared, cored and quartered cooking apples (about 4 pounds)

2 cups sugar

1 teaspoon ground ginger

1 teaspoon ground cinnamon

¹/₂ teaspoon ground cloves

Heat apple cider to boiling in 5-quart Dutch oven. Boil uncovered until cider measures 2 quarts, about 1¼ hours. Add apples. Heat to boiling: reduce heat. Simmer uncovered, stirring frequently, until apples are very soft, about 1 hour.

Press through sieve or food mill, or mash with potato masher just until smooth. Stir in remaining ingredients. Heat to boiling; reduce heat. Simmer uncovered, stirring frequently, until no liquid separates from pulp, about 2 hours. Heat to boiling.

Immediately pour mixture into hot sterilized jars, leaving ¼-inch headspace. Wipe rims of jars. Seal and process in boiling water bath 10 minutes. *About 3 half-pints butter.*

Nutrition Information Per Serving

1 tablespoon

Calories	95	Fat, g	0
Protein, g	0	Cholesterol, mg	0
Carbohydrate, g	24	Sodium, mg	0

Brandy Apple Butter

Brandy is a lovely way to dress up apple butter for gift giving or for use in cakes, pies and pastries. Preparing apple butter with brandy was customary to help keep it fresh in the days before paraffin. A round of tissue paper soaked in brandy was fitted over the top of the butter, and then covered. These days, some cooks in California add brandy, often locally produced. Our recipe is delicious whether or not you use brandy from California.

12 cups pared, cored and quartered cooking apples (about 4 pounds)

3 cups apple cider or juice

1 cup granulated sugar

1 cup packed brown sugar

1 cup brandy

1 teaspoon ground cinnamon

Heat apples and apple cider to boiling in Dutch oven or stockpot; reduce heat. Simmer uncovered, stirring frequently, until apples are very soft, about 1 hour.

Press through sieve or food mill, or mash with potato masher just until smooth. Return apple mixture to Dutch oven. Stir in remaining ingredients. Heat to boiling; reduce heat. Simmer uncovered, stirring frequently, until no liquid separates from pulp, about 2 hours.

Immediately pour mixture into hot, sterilized jars, leaving ¼-inch headspace. Wipe rims of jars. Seal and process in boiling water bath 10 minutes. *About 4 half-pints butter.*

Nutrition Information Per Serving

1 tablespoon

Calories	45	Fat, g	0
Protein, g	0	Cholesterol, mg	0
Carbohydrate, g	11	Sodium, mg	0

Corn Relish

Corn was an important year-round staple in the early days of this country. Pennsylvania Dutch and New England cooks preserved the corn harvest in this colorful relish. Midwestern cooks customized the recipe by including the cabbage that grew in abundance in their gardens. While we may no longer need to preserve food in this manner, you'll be taken with the beauty and fresh flavor of this lovely relish. The USDA recommends processing all relishes and pickles in a boiling water canner, as we do in this recipe.

9 ears corn

1¹/₂ cups sugar

3 tablespoons all-purpose flour

2 tablespoons pickling or uniodized salt

2 teaspoons dry mustard

1 teaspoon ground turmeric

3 cups white vinegar

3 medium onions, chopped (about 1¹/₂ cups)

2 medium red bell peppers, chopped (about 2 cups)

1 medium green bell pepper, chopped (about 1 cup)

1 small head green cabbage, chopped (about 3 cups)

Place corn in Dutch oven; add enough cold water to cover. Heat to boiling. Boil uncovered 3 minutes. Drain water from corn; cool. Cut enough kernels from corn to measure 5 cups.

Mix sugar, flour, salt, mustard and turmeric in Dutch oven; stir in vinegar. Heat to boiling; reduce heat. Add corn and remaining vegetables. Simmer uncovered 25 minutes. Immediately pack mixture in hot sterilized jars, leaving ¹/₄-inch headspace. Wipe rims of jars. Seal and process in boiling water bath 15 minutes. *About 5 pints relish.*

Nutrition Information Per Serving

1 tablespoon

Calories	30	Fat, g	0
Protein, g	1	Cholesterol, mg	0
Carbohydrate, g	8	Sodium, mg	165

Corn Relish, Sauerkraut Relish (page 93) and Apple Butter (page 86)

Bread and Butter Pickles

Crunchy, flavorful pickles are always a treat. Your search for the perfect pickle recipe ends here! Be sure to start with fresh, firm, slightly underripe cucumbers, so that you'll have wonderful crisp pickles. Cucumbers that are too ripe produce soft pickles. The soaking process is also critical to crispness, so follow it carefully. Noncaking ingredients added to table salt can make the brine cloudy, so use pickling (noniodized) salt, which you'll find next to regular salt in the grocery store.

3 quarts thinly sliced unpared cucumbers (about 4 pounds)

7 cups thinly sliced onions (about 2 pounds)

1 medium red bell pepper, cut into thin strips

1 medium green bell pepper, cut into thin strips

1/2 cup pickling or uniodized salt

2 1/2 cups sugar

2 1/2 cups cider or white vinegar

1 cup water

2 tablespoons mustard seed

1 teaspoon celery seed

1 teaspoon ground turmeric

Mix cucumbers, onions and peppers. Dissolve salt in water; pour over vegetables. Place a solid layer of ice cubes or crushed ice over vegetables. Weight with a heavy object and let stand 3 hours.

Drain vegetables thoroughly. Mix remaining ingredients; heat to boiling. Add vegetables; heat to boiling. Immediately pack mixture into hot sterilized jars, leaving 1/4-inch headspace. Wipe rims of jars. Seal and process in boiling water bath 10 minutes. *About 6 pints pickles.*

Nutrition Information Per Serving

1/4 cup

Calories	30	Fat, g	0
Protein, g	0	Cholesterol, mg	0
Carbohydrate, g	7	Sodium, mg	210

Spiced Peaches

The Pennsylvania Dutch are celebrated for serving "sweets and sours" at their tables— preserved fruits, vegetables and pickled combinations are all favorites. Spiced Peaches, with their luscious combination of ripe peaches, sweet brown sugar and zesty spices, are particularly popular. Serve them with meats, poultry and as a topping for sponge cake or shortbread.

> *3 cups packed brown sugar*
>
> *2 cups vinegar*
>
> *1 tablespoon whole cloves*
>
> *1 tablespoon whole allspice*
>
> *4 sticks cinnamon, broken into pieces*
>
> *5 pounds firm ripe peaches (about 15 peaches)*

Mix brown sugar and vinegar in 6-quart Dutch oven or stockpot. Tie cloves, allspice and cinnamon in cheesecloth bag; add to brown sugar mixture. Heat to boiling, stirring frequently; reduce heat. Simmer uncovered 30 minutes.

Place peaches in boiling water 30 to 60 seconds; immediately remove with slotted spoon and plunge into cold water. Slip off skins. Cut in half and remove pits. Add peaches to syrup. Cover and simmer until peaches are tender when pierced with fork, 5 to 10 minutes. Remove cheesecloth bag.

Pack peaches, cavity sides down, in hot sterilized wide-mouth jars.* Cover peaches with boiling syrup, leaving 1/2-inch headspace. Wipe rims of jars. Seal and process in boiling water bath 20 minutes for pint jars, 25 minutes for quart jars. *About 6 pints peaches.*

Nutrition Information Per Serving

1 peach

Calories	85	Fat, g	0
Protein, g	0	Cholesterol, mg	0
Carbohydrate, g	21	Sodium, mg	5

*Either pint or quart wide-mouth jars may be used.

Watermelon Pickles

¹/₄ cup pickling or uniodized salt

8 cups cold water

16 cups 1-inch cubes pared watermelon rind

2 tablespoons whole cloves

3 sticks cinnamon, broken into pieces

1 piece gingerroot

9 cups sugar

8 cups cider vinegar

Dissolve salt in cold water; pour over watermelon rind. Stir in additional water, if necessary, to cover rind. Let stand in cool place 8 hours.

Drain rind; cover with cold water. Heat to boiling. Cook uncovered just until tender, 10 to 15 minutes; drain. Tie cloves, cinnamon and gingerroot in cheesecloth bag. Heat cheesecloth bag, sugar and vinegar to boiling in Dutch oven, stirring occasionally. Boil uncovered 5 minutes; reduce heat. Add rind. Simmer uncovered 1 hour, stirring occasionally. Remove cheesecloth bag. Immediately pack mixture in hot sterilized jars, leaving ¹/₄-inch headspace. Wipe rims of jars. Seal and process in boiling water bath 10 minutes. *About 7 pints pickles.*

Nutrition Information Per Serving

¹/₄ cup

Calories	90	Fat, g	0
Protein, g	0	Cholesterol, mg	0
Carbohydrate, g	22	Sodium, mg	440

Sauerkraut Relish

¹/₂ cup sugar

1 medium red bell pepper, chopped (about 1 cup)

1 medium onion, chopped (about ¹/₂ cup)

1 medium stalk celery, sliced (about ¹/₂ cup)

1 medium carrot, coarsely shredded (about ¹/₂ cup)

1 jar or can (16 ounces) sauerkraut, undrained

Mix all ingredients in 2-quart glass or plastic bowl. Cover and refrigerate at least 8 hours but no longer than 1 week. *About 1 quart relish.*

Nutrition Information Per Serving

1 tablespoon

Calories	10	Fat, g	0
Protein, g	0	Cholesterol, mg	0
Carbohydrate, g	2	Sodium, mg	50

Watermelon Pickles

6

Favorite Sweets

Americans have a sweet tooth, and creating desserts and other sweet treats has been a pleasure for cooks across the country. Pies were an early, frugal use of fresh fruits, berries, nuts, dried fruits and even vegetables, such as sweet potatoes. Apple pies have become a classic, as well as the deep dish pie, invented to hold more succulent fruits and berries!

Cooks in a hurry developed cobblers, crisps and slumps, luscious ways to use fresh fruits in a flash. Cookies such as Joe Froggers and Snickerdoodles were welcome when served for lunch in the fields, or served at the table. And cakes such as Red Devil's Food Cake with Chocolate Frosting were savored on special occasions.

Today, everyone can enjoy regional favorites. Key Lime Pie, Kentucky Pecan Pie, Pralines and other delicious items are easy to make at home whenever you'd like, not just to be sampled while traveling. You'll also enjoy our collection of apple pie recipes from around the country, sure to spark some new baking ideas.

Lemon-filled Coconut Cake (page 96)

Lemon-filled Coconut Cake

Lemon Filling (below)
2¼ cups all-purpose flour
1⅔ cups granulated sugar
⅔ cup shortening
1¼ cups milk
3½ teaspoons baking powder
1 teaspoon salt
1 teaspoon vanilla
5 egg whites
1 cup flaked or shredded coconut
1 cup whipping (heavy) cream
¼ cup powdered sugar

Prepare Lemon Filling; press plastic wrap onto hot filling. Refrigerate until set, about 1 hour.

Heat oven to 350°. Grease and flour 2 round pans, 8 × 1½ or 9 × 1½ inches. Beat flour, granulated sugar, shortening, milk, baking powder, salt and vanilla in 3-quart bowl on low speed, scraping bowl constantly, 30 seconds. Beat on high speed, scraping bowl occasionally, 2 minutes. Beat in egg whites on high speed, scraping bowl occasionally, 2 minutes. Stir in coconut. Pour into pans.

Bake until toothpick inserted in center comes out clean or top springs back when touched lightly, 30 to 35 minutes. Cool 10 minutes; remove from pans. Cool completely on wire rack.

Beat whipping cream and powdered sugar in chilled 1½-quart bowl until stiff. Fill layers with Lemon Filling and frost with whipped cream; refrigerate. Immediately refrigerate any remaining cake. *16 servings.*

LEMON FILLING

¾ cup sugar
3 tablespoons cornstarch
¼ teaspoon salt
¾ cup water
1 tablespoon margarine or butter
1 teaspoon finely grated lemon peel
⅓ cup lemon juice
2 to 4 drops yellow food color, if desired

Mix sugar, cornstarch and salt in 1½-quart saucepan. Gradually stir in water. Cook over medium heat, stirring constantly, until mixture thickens and boils. Boil and stir 5 minutes; remove from heat. Stir in margarine and lemon peel until margarine is melted. Gradually stir in lemon juice and food color.

Nutrition Information Per Serving

1 serving

Calories	360	Fat, g	16
Protein, g	4	Cholesterol, mg	20
Carbohydrate, g	50	Sodium, mg	300

Red Devil's Food Cake

*1²/₃ cups all-purpose flour or 2 cups
  cake flour*

1 cup granulated sugar

¹/₂ cup packed brown sugar

¹/₂ cup shortening

1¹/₂ cups buttermilk

1¹/₂ teaspoons baking soda

1 teaspoon salt

1 teaspoon vanilla

2 eggs

*2 ounces unsweetened chocolate, melted
  and cooled*

*Creamy Vanilla Frosting or Chocolate
  Frosting (below), if desired*

Heat oven to 350°. Grease and flour 2 round pans, 8 × 1¹/₂ or 9 × 1¹/₂ inches, or rectangular pan, 13 × 9 × 2 inches. Beat all ingredients except frosting on low speed, scraping bowl constantly, 30 seconds. Beat on high speed, scraping bowl occasionally, 3 minutes. Pour into pan(s).

Bake until toothpick inserted in center comes out clean, layers 30 to 35 minutes, rectangle 35 to 40 minutes. Cool layers 10 minutes; remove from pans. Cool completely on wire rack. Fill and frost layers or frost top of rectangle with frosting. *16 servings*.

CREAMY VANILLA FROSTING

3 cups powdered sugar
¹/₃ cup margarine or butter, softened
1¹/₂ teaspoons vanilla
About 2 tablespoons milk

Mix powdered sugar and margarine. Stir in vanilla and milk; beat until smooth and of spreading consistency.

CHOCOLATE FROSTING

¹/₃ cup margarine or butter, softened
*2 ounces unsweetened chocolate, melted
  and cooled*
2 cups powdered sugar
1¹/₂ teaspoons vanilla
About 2 tablespoons milk

Mix margarine and chocolate. Stir in powdered sugar. Beat in vanilla and milk until smooth and of spreading consistency.

Nutrition Information Per Serving

1 serving

Calories	350	Fat, g	13
Protein, g	3	Cholesterol, mg	30
Carbohydrate, g	55	Sodium, mg	290

Raspberry Jam Cake

Southwesterners are particularly fond of traditional southern cakes, such as this spice-laden jam cake. You'll find that blackberry is the jam of choice in Texas and the western states, but in the Appalachian Mountain region, raspberry is the favorite. One thing everyone agrees on is that the buttery caramel frosting is just perfect! This rich, dense cake keeps well for several days, so it's easy to have on hand when neighbors and friends drop by to chat over a cup of coffee.

*1 cup (2 sticks) margarine or butter,
    softened*

¹/₂ cup granulated sugar

¹/₂ cup packed brown sugar

4 eggs

*1 jar (10 ounces) red raspberry pre-
    serves (about 1 cup)*

3¹/₄ cups all-purpose flour

1 teaspoon baking powder

1 teaspoon baking soda

1 teaspoon ground nutmeg

1 teaspoon ground cinnamon

¹/₂ teaspoon salt

¹/₄ teaspoon ground cloves

1 cup buttermilk

1 cup chopped pecans

Caramel Frosting (below)

Heat oven to 350°. Grease and flour tube pan, 10 × 4 inches. Beat margarine and sugars in 3-quart bowl on medium speed, scraping bowl constantly, until blended. Beat on high speed 1 minute. Beat in eggs and preserves until well blended. (Mixture will appear curdled.) Beat in flour, baking powder, baking soda, nutmeg, cinnamon, salt, and cloves alternately with buttermilk, beginning and ending with flour mixture, until well blended. Stir in pecans. Pour into pan.

Bake until toothpick inserted in center comes out clean and top springs back when touched lightly, 70 to 75 minutes. Cool 10 minutes; remove from pan. Cool completely on wire rack. Frost with Caramel Frosting. *16 servings.*

CARAMEL FROSTING

¹/₂ cup (1 stick) margarine or butter
1 cup packed brown sugar
¹/₄ cup milk
2 cups powdered sugar

Heat margarine in 2-quart saucepan until melted. Stir in brown sugar. Heat to boiling, stirring constantly. Boil and stir over low heat 2 minutes; stir in milk. Heat to boiling; remove from heat. Cool to lukewarm. Gradually stir in powdered sugar; beat until smooth and of spreading consistency. If frosting becomes too stiff, stir in additional milk, 1 teaspoon at a time.

Nutrition Information Per Serving

1 serving			
Calories	545	Fat, g	24
Protein, g	5	Cholesterol, mg	55
Carbohydrate, g	77	Sodium, mg	390

Pineapple Upside-down Cake

¹/₄ cup (¹/₂ stick) margarine or butter

1 can (20 ounces) sliced pineapple in syrup, drained (reserve 2 tablespoons syrup)

²/₃ cup packed brown sugar

Maraschino cherries, if desired

1¹/₂ cups cake flour or 1¹/₄ cups all-purpose flour

1 cup granulated sugar

¹/₃ cup shortening

³/₄ cup milk

1¹/₂ teaspoons baking powder

1 teaspoon vanilla

¹/₂ teaspoon salt

1 egg

Sweetened whipped cream

Heat oven to 350°. Heat margarine in 9-inch ovenproof skillet or square pan, 9 × 9 × 2 inches, in oven until melted. Stir reserved pineapple syrup into margarine; sprinkle evenly with brown sugar. Arrange pineapple slices in margarine mixture. Place cherry in center of each pineapple slice, if desired.

Beat remaining ingredients except whipped cream in 3-quart bowl on low speed, scraping bowl constantly, 30 seconds. Beat on high speed, scraping bowl occasionally, 3 minutes. Pour evenly over pineapple slices. Bake until toothpick inserted in center comes out clean, 40 to 45 minutes. Invert on heatproof platter. Leave skillet over cake a few minutes. Serve warm with whipped cream. *9 servings.*

APRICOT UPSIDE-DOWN CAKE: Substitute 1 can (17 ounces) apricot halves for the pineapple slices.

PEACH UPSIDE-DOWN CAKE: Substitute 1 can (16 ounces) sliced peaches for the pineapple slices.

PLUM UPSIDE-DOWN CAKE: Substitute 1 can (17 ounces) plums, cut in half and pitted, for the pineapple slices.

Nutrition Information Per Serving

1 serving

Calories	425	Fat, g	18
Protein, g	3	Cholesterol, mg	45
Carbohydrate, g	63	Sodium, mg	270

Orchard Squares

Toasted Almond Pastry (below)

¹/₃ to ²/₃ cup granulated sugar

¹/₃ cup all-purpose flour

¹/₂ teaspoon ground nutmeg

Dash of salt

3 cups sliced fresh peaches (about 3 medium)

3 cups sliced fresh pears (about 3 medium)

2 cups thinly sliced pared tart apples (about 2 medium)

2 tablespoons lemon juice

2 tablespoons margarine or butter

³/₄ cup powdered sugar

About 1 tablespoon milk or lemon juice

Prepare Toasted Almond Pastry. Gather into a ball; cut in half. Shape each half into flattened round on lightly floured cloth-covered surface. Roll 1 round into rectangle, 18 × 13 inches, with floured cloth-covered rolling pin. Fold pastry into quarters; unfold and ease into ungreased jelly roll pan, 15¹/₂ × 10¹/₂ × 1 inch.

Heat oven to 425°. Mix granulated sugar, flour, nutmeg and salt in large bowl. Stir in fruit. Turn into pastry-lined pan. Drizzle lemon juice over fruit. Dot with margarine. Roll other round pastry into rectangle, 17 × 12 inches. Fold into quarters; cut slits so steam can escape. Place on fruit mixture and unfold; seal and flute.

Bake until crust is brown and juice begins to bubble through slits in crust, 35 to 40 minutes; cool slightly. Mix powdered sugar and milk until smooth; drizzle over crust. Cut into about 3-inch squares. Serve warm with ice cream if desired. *15 servings.*

TOASTED ALMOND PASTRY

1¹/₄ cups shortening
3¹/₂ cups all-purpose flour
¹/₄ cup ground toasted almonds
1 teaspoon salt
8 to 9 tablespoons cold water

Cut shortening into flour, almonds and salt until particles are size of small peas. Sprinkle in water, 1 tablespoon at a time, tossing with fork until all flour is moistened and pastry almost cleans side of bowl (1 to 2 teaspoons water can be added if necessary).

Nutrition Information Per Serving

1 serving			
Calories	385	Fat, g	20
Protein, g	4	Cholesterol, mg	0
Carbohydrate, g	47	Sodium, mg	180

Orchard Squares, Honey Walnut Pie
(page 103)

Kentucky Pecan Pie

Pastry for 9-inch one-crust pie (below)

²/₃ cup sugar

¹/₃ cup margarine or butter, melted

1 cup corn syrup

2 tablespoons bourbon, if desired

¹/₂ teaspoon salt

3 eggs

1 cup pecan halves or broken pecans

1 cup semisweet chocolate chips

Heat oven to 375°. Prepare Pastry. Beat sugar, margarine, corn syrup, bourbon, if desired, salt and eggs with hand beater. Stir in pecans and chocolate chips. Pour into pastry-lined pie plate. Cover edge with 2- to 3-inch strip of aluminum foil to prevent excessive browning; remove foil last 15 minutes of baking. Bake until set, 40 to 50 minutes. Refrigerate until chilled, at least 2 hours. Immediately refrigerate any remaining pie. *8 servings*.

ONE-CRUST PIE PASTRY

*¹/₃ cup plus 1 tablespoon shortening or
¹/₃ cup lard*

1 cup all-purpose flour

¹/₂ teaspoon salt

2 to 3 tablespoons cold water

Cut shortening into flour and salt until particles are size of small peas. Sprinkle in water, 1 tablespoon at a time, tossing with fork until all flour is moistened and pastry almost cleans side of bowl (1 to 2 teaspoons water can be added if necessary).

Gather pastry into a ball; shape into flattened round on lightly floured cloth-covered board. Roll pastry 2 inches larger than inverted pie plate. Fold pastry into fourths and place in pie plate with point in center; unfold. Trim overhanging edge of pastry 1 inch from rim of pie plate. Fold and roll pastry under even with pie plate; flute.

CHOCOLATE PECAN PIE: Melt 2 ounces unsweetened chocolate with the margarine. Omit bourbon and chocolate chips.

PEANUT–CHOCOLATE CHIP PIE: Omit bourbon and 1 cup chocolate chips from filling. Substitute 1 cup salted peanuts for the pecans. After baking, sprinkle with ¹/₂ cup semisweet chocolate chips. Let stand 30 minutes before refrigerating.

PECAN PIE: Omit bourbon and chocolate chips.

Nutrition Information Per Serving

1 serving

Calories	615	Fat, g	33
Protein, g	6	Cholesterol, mg	80
Carbohydrate, g	73	Sodium, mg	420

Lemon-Coconut Pie

2 large lemons

1 cup sugar

1 teaspoon salt

Pastry for 9-inch one-crust pie (page 102)

4 eggs

1 cup corn syrup

1 cup shredded coconut

1 cup whipped (heavy) cream

Grate peel from lemons to measure 2 teaspoons. Pare lemons, removing all white membrane. Cut lemons into very thin slices. Sprinkle lemon peel, sugar and salt over lemon slices; let stand at room temperature 2 hours.

Heat oven to 375°. Prepare Pastry. Beat eggs and corn syrup; stir in coconut. Pour coconut mixture over lemon slices; mix well. Pour into pastry-lined pie plate. Cover edge with 2- to 3-inch strip of aluminum foil to prevent excess browning; remove foil during last 15 minutes of baking.

Bake until filling is set and pastry is golden brown, 40 to 50 minutes. Refrigerate until cold, at least 6 hours but no longer than 24 hours. Serve with whipped cream, and if desired, garnish with lemon peel or slices. Refrigerate any remaining pie. *8 servings.*

Nutrition Information Per Serving

1 serving

Calories	520	Fat, g	22
Protein, g	6	Cholesterol, mg	110
Carbohydrate, g	74	Sodium, mg	430

Honey Walnut Pie

Pastry for 9-inch one-crust pie (page 102)

¹/₂ cup packed brown sugar

¹/₂ cup corn syrup

¹/₂ cup honey

1 tablespoon all-purpose flour

1 tablespoon margarine or butter, melted

1 teaspoon vanilla

¹/₄ teaspoon salt

2 eggs

1¹/₂ cups walnut pieces

Heat oven to 350°. Prepare Pastry. Beat brown sugar, corn syrup, honey, flour, margarine, vanilla, salt and eggs with hand beater. Stir in walnuts. Pour into pastry-lined pie plate. Cover edge with 2-inch strip of aluminum foil to prevent excessive browning; remove foil last 15 minutes of baking. Bake until set, 45 to 55 minutes. Refrigerate until chilled, at least 2 hours. Immediately refrigerate any remaining pie. *8 servings.*

Nutrition Information Per Serving

1 serving

Calories	495	Fat, g	25
Protein, g	6	Cholesterol, mg	55
Carbohydrate, g	61	Sodium, mg	270

Sweet Potato Pie

Pastry for 9-inch one-crust pie (page 102)

2 eggs

³/4 cup sugar

1 teaspoon ground cinnamon

¹/2 teaspoon salt

¹/2 teaspoon ground ginger

¹/4 teaspoon ground cloves

1 can (23 ounces) sweet potatoes, drained and mashed (1³/4 to 2 cups)

1 can (12 ounces) evaporated milk

Sweetened whipped cream, if desired

Heat oven to 425°. Prepare Pastry. Beat eggs slightly in 2-quart bowl with hand beater; beat in remaining ingredients except whipped cream. Place pastry-lined pie plate on oven rack; pour sweet potato mixture into plate. Cover edge with 2-inch strip of aluminum foil to prevent excessive browning; remove foil last 15 minutes of baking. Bake 15 minutes.

Reduce oven temperature to 350°. Bake until knife inserted in center comes out clean, 45 to 50 minutes. Refrigerate until chilled, at least 4 hours. Serve with sweetened whipped cream, if desired. Immediately refrigerate any remaining pie. *8 servings*.

PRALINE SWEET POTATO PIE: Decrease second baking time to 35 minutes. Mix ¹/3 cup packed brown sugar, ¹/3 cup chopped pecans and 1 tablespoon margarine or butter, softened; sprinkle over pie. Bake until knife inserted in center comes out clean, about 10 minutes longer.

PUMPKIN PIE: Substitute 1 can (16 ounces) pumpkin for the sweet potatoes.

Nutrition Information Per Serving

1 serving

Calories	355	Fat, g	13
Protein, g	7	Cholesterol, mg	65
Carbohydrate, g	53	Sodium, mg	370

Key Lime Pie

Key Lime Pie hails from the Florida Keys, which is the only place where the special yellow Key limes will grow. But you don't have to go to Florida to pick your own limes; regular lemons and limes will also make a delicious pie. Sweetened condensed milk is the "key" to the wonderful creamy texture of this nationwide favorite.

1 can (14 ounces) sweetened condensed milk

1 tablespoon grated lemon peel

$1/2$ teaspoon grated lime peel

$1/4$ cup lemon juice

$1/4$ cup lime juice

3 or 4 drops green food color

3 eggs, separated

$1/4$ teaspoon cream of tartar

9-inch baked pie shell (below)

Mix milk, lemon peel, lime peel, lemon juice, lime juice and food color. Beat egg yolks slightly; stir in milk mixture. Beat egg whites and cream of tartar in $2^{1}/_2$-quart bowl until stiff and glossy. Fold egg yolk mixture into egg whites; mound in pie shell. Refrigerate until set, at least 2 hours. Garnish with sweetened whipped cream and grated lime peel, if desired. Immediately refrigerate any remaining pie. *8 servings*.

BAKED ONE-CRUST PIE SHELL

$1/3$ cup plus 1 tablespoon shortening or $1/3$ cup lard

1 cup all-purpose flour

$1/2$ teaspoon salt

2 to 3 tablespoons cold water

Heat oven to 475°. Cut shortening into flour and salt until particles are size of small peas. Sprinkle in water, 1 tablespoon at a time, tossing with fork until all flour is moistened and pastry almost cleans side of bowl (1 to 2 teaspoons water can be added if necessary).

Gather pastry into a ball; shape into flattened round on lightly floured cloth-covered board. Roll pastry 2 inches larger than inverted pie plate. Fold pastry into fourths and place in pie plate with point in center; unfold. Trim overhanging edge of pastry 1 inch from rim of pie plate. Fold and roll pastry under even with pie plate; flute. Prick bottom and side thoroughly with fork to prevent puffing while baking. Bake 8 to 10 minutes or until light brown; cool.

Nutrition Information Per Serving

1 serving

Calories	305	Fat, g	14
Protein, g	7	Cholesterol, mg	95
Carbohydrate, g	38	Sodium, mg	240

All-American Apple Pies ✴✴✴✴✴

Apple pie is an American variation of a British favorite. In fact, it was a classic in England long before the Pilgrims ever came to America. These early British pies were different, however. They were generally square or oblong, and deeper than the pies we bake now. Early New England colonists stretched their food supplies by changing the shape of pie pans to the style we use today. Shallow and slant-sided, the new pans needed fewer apples to make a pie that was still hearty and delicious. The colonists didn't always have an apple surplus, because the young trees that they planted had to produce enough fruit to last throughout the year. So, even though apple pies were popular in Britain too, the phrase "as American as apple pie" indeed has merit because the shallow, double-crusted pie we make is uniquely American.

Deep-dish Apple Pie

Our Deep-dish Apple Pie is typical of the British-style pie, sometimes known as a cobbler. Midwestern farmers have made deep-dish pies for generations. Because they require more fruit, deep-dish pies are an excellent way to put an overabundance of perishable fresh fruit to good use.

Pastry (below)

1¹/₂ cups sugar

¹/₂ cup all-purpose flour

1 teaspoon ground nutmeg

1 teaspoon ground cinnamon

¹/₄ teaspoon salt

*12 cups thinly sliced pared tart apples
(about 11 medium)*

2 tablespoons margarine or butter

Heat oven to 425°. Prepare Pastry. Mix sugar, flour, nutmeg, cinnamon and salt. Stir in apples. Turn into ungreased square pan, 9 × 9 × 2 inches. Dot with margarine. Cover with crust; fold edges under just inside edges of pan. Cut slits near center so steam can escape. Bake until juice begins to bubble through slits in crust, about 1 hour. Serve slightly warm. *12 servings.*

PASTRY

1 cup all-purpose flour

¹/₂ teaspoon salt

*¹/₃ cup plus 1 tablespoon shortening or
¹/₃ cup lard*

2 to 3 tablespoons cold water

Mix flour and salt. Cut in shortening until particles are size of small peas. Sprinkle in water, 1 tablespoon at a time, tossing with fork until all flour is moistened and pastry almost cleans side of bowl (1 to 2 teaspoons water can be added if necessary). Gather pastry into ball; shape into flattened round on slightly floured cloth-covered board. Roll into 10-inch square with floured cloth-covered rolling pin.

Nutrition Information Per Serving

1 serving

Calories	295	Fat, g	9
Protein, g	2	Cholesterol, mg	0
Carbohydrate, g	52	Sodium, mg	155

✴✴✴✴✴✴✴✴✴✴✴✴✴✴✴✴✴✴✴✴

Apple-Praline Pie

Our recipe for Apple-Praline Pie comes from Louisiana. This indulgent dessert combines apples and pecans between two pastry crusts, and it's all covered with a luscious praline glaze.

Pastry for 10-inch two-crust pie

1 cup granulated sugar

1 cup chopped pecans

1/3 cup all-purpose flour

1 teaspoon ground cinnamon

1 teaspoon ground nutmeg

1/4 teaspoon salt

8 cups thinly sliced pared tart apples (about 7 medium)

3 tablespoons margarine or butter

1/4 cup packed brown sugar

2 tablespoons half-and-half

Heat oven to 425°. Prepare Pastry. Mix granulated sugar, 2/3 cup of the pecans, flour, cinnamon, nutmeg and salt in large bowl. Toss with apples. Turn into pastry-lined pie plate. Dot with margarine. Cover with top crust that has slits cut in it; seal and flute. Cover edge with 2- to 3-inch strip of aluminum foil to prevent excessive browning; remove foil during last 15 minutes of baking. Bake until crust is brown and juice begins to bubble through slits in crust, 50 to 60 minutes.

Mix brown sugar, remaining pecans and the half-and-half in 1-quart saucepan. Cook over low heat, stirring constantly, until sugar is melted. Spread over hot pie. *8 servings.*

Nutrition Information Per Serving

1 serving			
Calories	615	Fat, g	33
Protein, g	5	Cholesterol, mg	15
Carbohydrate, g	75	Sodium, mg	430

Cranberry-Apple Pie

Cranberries' tart flavor and beautiful color have made them natural additions to apple pies. Although Cape Cod produces the most cranberries, Washington State is known for the high quality of its own plump, juicy berries. Combine cranberries with old-fashioned Northwestern apple varieties such as Gravenstein, Criterion and Granny Smith. Bakers across America like to combine different varieties of apples in their pies. No matter which varieties you choose, be sure to use apples that are firm and tart.

Pastry for 9-inch two-crust pie

1 3/4 cups sugar

1/4 cup all-purpose flour

3 cups sliced pared tart apples (3 medium)

2 cups fresh or thawed frozen cranberries

2 tablespoons margarine or butter

Heat oven to 425°. Prepare Pastry. Mix sugar and flour. In pastry-lined pie plate, alternate layers of apples, cranberries and sugar mixture, beginning and ending with apples. Dot with margarine. Cover with top crust that has slits cut in it; seal and flute. Cover edge with 2- to 3-inch strip of aluminum foil to prevent excessive browning; remove foil last 15 minutes of baking. Bake until crust is brown, 40 to 50 minutes. Cool. *8 servings.*

Nutrition Information Per Serving

1 serving			
Calories	475	Fat, g	19
Protein, g	3	Cholesterol, mg	10
Carbohydrate, g	73	Sodium, mg	310

Black Bottom Pie

Starting at the turn of the twentieth century, Black Bottom Pies have been served in the South at special occasions. This triple-tiered treat of rich chocolate, smooth rum-flavored custard and whipped cream piled in a gingery crust is sure to be a hit no matter where it is served.

Gingersnap Crust (below)
½ cup granulated sugar
2 tablespoons cornstarch
¼ teaspoon salt
2 cups milk
3 egg yolks
1 teaspoon vanilla
1 envelope unflavored gelatin
¼ cup cold water
1 to 2 tablespoons rum or 1 teaspoon rum flavoring
3 ounces semisweet chocolate, melted and cooled
3 egg whites
¼ teaspoon cream of tartar
⅓ cup granulated sugar
1 cup whipping (heavy) cream
2 tablespoons powdered sugar

Bake Gingersnap Crust; cool. Mix ½ cup granulated sugar, the cornstarch and salt in 2-quart saucepan. Mix milk and egg yolks; gradually stir into sugar mixture. Cook over medium heat, stirring constantly, until mixture thickens and boils. Boil and stir 1 minute. Stir in vanilla. remove 1 cup of the custard mixture; reserve.

Sprinkle gelatin on cold water to soften; stir into custard mixture in pan until gelatin is dissolved. Stir in rum. Refrigerate, stirring occasionally, until mixture mounds when dropped from a spoon, about 10 minutes.

Mix chocolate and reserved custard mixture; pour into crust. Beat egg whites and cream of tartar in 2½-quart bowl until foamy. Beat in ⅓ cup granulated sugar, 1 tablespoon at a time; continue beating until stiff and glossy. Do not underbeat. Fold remaining custard mixture into meringue; spread over chocolate mixture. Refrigerate until set, at least 3 hours.

Beat whipping cream and powdered sugar in chilled 1½-quart bowl until stiff. Spread over pie. Sprinkle with ground nutmeg, if desired. Immediately refrigerate any remaining pie. *8 servings*.

GINGERSNAP CRUST

1½ cups crushed gingersnaps (about 22)
¼ cup (½ stick) margarine or butter, melted

Heat oven to 350°. Mix gingersnaps and margarine. Press firmly and evenly against bottom and side of ungreased pie plate, 9 × 1¼ inches. Bake 10 minutes.

Nutrition Information Per Serving

1 serving			
Calories	525	Fat, g	27
Protein, g	8	Cholesterol, mg	115
Carbohydrate, g	63	Sodium, mg	420

Citrus-Peach Shortcakes

Shortcakes are an all-American dessert that showcases the fruits of the summer harvest. In days gone by, shortcake was usually the size of a breakfast plate. While we keep the traditional rich baking powder biscuit base, our recipe makes individual shortcakes. But we have remained true to the custom of filling the shortcake with sweet fresh fruit, and topping it with mounds of luscious whipped cream.

> *4 cups sliced pared peaches (about 2 pounds)*
>
> *1 cup sugar*
>
> *Citrus Glaze (below)*
>
> *2 cups all-purpose flour*
>
> *2 tablespoons sugar*
>
> *3 teaspoons baking powder*
>
> *1/2 teaspoon salt*
>
> *1 tablespoon grated orange peel*
>
> *1/3 cup shortening*
>
> *3/4 cup milk*
>
> *Margarine or butter*
>
> *Sweetened whipped cream*

Mix peaches and 1 cup sugar; let stand 1 hour. Prepare Citrus Glaze.

Heat oven to 450°. Mix flour, 2 tablespoons sugar, the baking powder and salt in 2-quart bowl. Mix in orange peel. Cut in shortening until mixture resembles fine crumbs. Stir in milk just until blended. Gently smooth dough into ball on lightly floured cloth-covered surface; knead 20 to 25 times. Pat or roll about 1/4 inch thick; cut into 12 rounds with floured 3-inch cutter. Dot half of the rounds with margarine; top with remaining rounds. Place about 1 inch apart on ungreased cookie sheet. Bake until golden brown, 12 to 15 minutes.

Split shortcakes in half while hot. Fill and top with peaches; drizzle with glaze. Top with whipped cream. *6 servings.*

CITRUS GLAZE

> *1 cup sugar*
>
> *1/3 cup orange juice*
>
> *1 tablespoon grated orange peel*
>
> *3 tablespoons lemon juice*
>
> *1 teaspoon light corn syrup*

Heat all ingredients to boiling in 1-quart saucepan. Reduce heat. Simmer until mixture thickens slightly, about 15 minutes. Cool.

Nutrition Information Per Serving

1 serving			
Calories	650	Fat, g	17
Protein, g	6	Cholesterol, mg	10
Carbohydrate, g	118	Sodium, mg	410

Blackberry Cobbler

Cobblers—popular throughout the United States—were so named because they could be made quickly, or "cobbled together." In the West, blackberry is the fruit of choice under a biscuitlike batter. The Northwest, where juicy blackberries still grow wild, is the home of this cobbler recipe.

4 cups fresh blackberries or raspberries

1 cup sugar

1 tablespoon cornstarch

½ teaspoon lemon juice

1 cup all-purpose flour

2 teaspoons baking powder

½ teaspoon salt

½ cup milk

¼ cup (½ stick) margarine or butter, melted

1 egg

Sweetened whipped cream or heavy cream, if desired

Heat oven to 375°. Place blackberries in 2-quart ungreased casserole. Reserve 1 teaspoon of the sugar. Mix remaining sugar, the cornstarch and lemon juice. Drizzle cornstarch mixture over blackberries; stir gently.

Mix flour, baking powder and salt in 2-quart bowl. Stir in milk, margarine and egg. Spread batter evenly over blackberries, sealing edge. Sprinkle with reserved sugar. Bake uncovered until topping is golden brown, 30 to 35 minutes. Let stand 10 minutes before serving. Serve with whipped cream, if desired. *8 servings.*

Nutrition Information Per Serving

1 serving

Calories	240	Fat, g	7
Protein, g	3	Cholesterol, mg	30
Carbohydrate, g	41	Sodium, mg	260

Blueberry Slump

½ cup sugar

2 tablespoons cornstarch

½ cup water

1 teaspoon lemon juice

4 cups blueberries

1 cup all-purpose flour

2 tablespoons sugar

1½ teaspoons baking powder

¼ teaspoon salt

¼ teaspoon ground nutmeg

¼ cup (½ stick) margarine or butter

⅓ cup milk

Cream

Mix ½ cup sugar and the cornstarch in 3-quart saucepan. Stir in water and lemon juice until well blended. Stir in blueberries. Cook over medium heat, stirring constantly, until mixture thickens and boils. Boil and stir 1 minute.

Mix flour, 2 tablespoons sugar, the baking powder, salt and nutmeg. Cut in margarine until mixture resembles fine crumbs. Stir in milk. Drop dough by 6 spoonfuls onto hot blueberry mixture. Cook uncovered over low heat 10 minutes; cover and cook 10 minutes longer. Serve hot with cream. *6 servings.*

Nutrition Information Per Serving

1 serving

Calories	420	Fat, g	20
Protein, g	5	Cholesterol, mg	40
Carbohydrate, g	55	Sodium, mg	310

Blueberry Slump, Cranberry-Apple Pie (page 107)

Strawberry Ice Cream

3 egg yolks, beaten

½ cup sugar

1 cup milk

¼ teaspoon salt

2 cups whipping (heavy) cream

1 teaspoon vanilla

1 pint strawberries

½ cup sugar

Few drops red food color, if desired

Mix egg yolks, ½ cup sugar, the milk and salt in 2-quart saucepan. Cook over medium heat, stirring constantly, just until bubbles appear around edge. Refrigerate in chilled bowl until room temperature, 2 to 3 hours.

Stir whipping cream and vanilla into milk mixture. Mash strawberries and ½ cup sugar; stir into milk mixture. Mix in food color, if desired. Pour into freezer can; put dasher in place. Cover and adjust crank. Place can in freezer tub. Fill freezer tub one-third full of ice; add remaining ice alternately with layers of rock salt (6 parts ice to 1 part rock salt). Turn crank until it turns with difficulty. Drain water from freezer tub. Remove lid; take out dasher. Pack mixture down; replace lid. Repack in ice and rock salt. Let stand several hours to ripen. *1 quart ice cream.*

CHOCOLATE ICE CREAM: Omit strawberries, ½ cup sugar and the food color. Increase sugar in cooked mixture to 1 cup. Beat 2 ounces unsweetened chocolate, melted, into milk mixture before cooking.

NUT BRITTLE ICE CREAM: Omit strawberries, ½ cup sugar and the food color. Increase vanilla to 1 tablespoon. Stir 1 cup crushed almond, pecan or peanut brittle into milk mixture after adding vanilla.

PEACH ICE CREAM: Omit strawberries and food color. Mash 4 or 5 peaches to yield 2 cups. Stir ½ cup sugar into peaches; stir into milk mixture after adding vanilla.

VANILLA BEAN ICE CREAM: Omit vanilla, strawberries, ½ cup sugar and food color. Add 3-inch piece of vanilla bean to milk mixture before cooking. Before cooling, remove bean and split lengthwise into halves. Scrape seeds into cooked mixture with tip of small knife; discard bean.

VANILLA ICE CREAM: Omit strawberries, ½ cup sugar and the food color. Increase vanilla to 1 tablespoon.

Nutrition Information Per Serving

½ cup

Calories	320	Fat, g	21
Protein, g	3	Cholesterol, mg	150
Carbohydrate, g	30	Sodium, mg	105

Rhubarb Crisp

1¹/₃ cups granulated sugar

¹/₃ cup all-purpose flour

¹/₂ teaspoon grated orange peel

4 cups ¹/₂-inch pieces fresh rhubarb or 1 package (16 ounces) frozen rhubarb, thawed and well drained (about 2 cups)

¹/₂ cup all-purpose flour

¹/₄ cup packed brown sugar

¹/₄ cup (¹/₂ stick) margarine or butter, softened

Heat oven to 400°. Mix granulated sugar, ¹/₃ cup flour and the orange peel; toss with rhubarb until well coated. Arrange rhubarb mixture in greased square pan, 8 × 8 × 2 inches. Sprinkle any remaining sugar mixture evenly over top.

Mix ¹/₂ cup flour, the brown sugar and margarine with fork until crumbly. Sprinkle evenly over rhubarb mixture. Bake until topping is golden brown and rhubarb is tender, 35 to 40 minutes. Serve warm with ice cream or whipped cream, if desired. *9 servings.*

Nutrition Information Per Serving

1 serving

Calories	230	Fat, g	5
Protein, g	1	Cholesterol, mg	0
Carbohydrate, g	45	Sodium, mg	65

Creamy Rice Pudding

When cold weather sets in, our thoughts turn to roaring fires, cozy get-togethers and comfort foods. Rice and plump raisins suspended in a rich custard make for one of the best winter desserts we know. The related baked rice custard (*sopa*) is often served by Hispanics in the Southwest.

²/₃ cup uncooked regular long grain rice

1¹/₃ cups water

2 eggs or 4 egg yolks

¹/₂ cup sugar

¹/₂ cup raisins

2 cups milk

¹/₂ teaspoon vanilla or 1 tablespoon grated orange peel

¹/₄ teaspoon salt

Ground nutmeg

Heat rice and water to boiling, stirring once or twice; reduce heat. Cover and simmer 14 minutes. (Do not lift cover or stir.) All water should be absorbed.

Heat oven to 325°. Beat eggs in ungreased 1¹/₂-quart casserole. Stir in sugar, raisins, milk, vanilla, salt and hot rice; sprinkle with nutmeg. Bake uncovered, stirring occasionally, until knife inserted halfway between center and edge comes out clean, 50 to 60 minutes. Serve warm or cold and, if desired, with cream. Immediately refrigerate any remaining pudding. *6 servings.*

Nutrition Information Per Serving

1 serving

Calories	250	Fat, g	4
Protein, g	6	Cholesterol, mg	75
Carbohydrate, g	47	Sodium, mg	155

Bread Pudding with Whiskey Sauce

Besides being delicious, Bread Pudding is popular all over the world because it makes delectable use of leftover bread that might otherwise go to waste. Early settlers frequently made Bread Pudding in the spring, when cows with calves produced more milk. Southern hospitality often calls for dessert recipes using fine old sherry or bourbon—this is especially true of Louisiana, the birthplace of this gently spiked Bread Pudding.

2 cups milk

1/4 cup (1/2 stick) margarine or butter

1/2 cup sugar

1 teaspoon ground cinnamon or nutmeg

1/4 teaspoon salt

2 eggs, slightly beaten

6 cups dry bread cubes (about 8 slices bread)

1/2 cup raisins, if desired

Whiskey Sauce or Amber Sauce (below)

Heat oven to 350°. Heat milk and margarine over medium heat until margarine is melted and milk is scalded. Mix sugar, cinnamon, salt and eggs in 4-quart bowl; stir in bread cubes and raisins. Stir in milk mixture; pour into ungreased 1½-quart casserole. Place casserole in pan of very hot water (1 inch deep). Bake uncovered until knife inserted 1 inch from edge of casserole comes out clean, 40 to 45 minutes. Prepare Whiskey or Amber Sauce; serve over warm bread pudding. *8 servings.*

WHISKEY SAUCE

1 cup packed brown sugar
1/2 cup (1 stick) margarine or butter
3 to 4 tablespoons bourbon

Heat all ingredients to boiling in 1-quart heavy saucepan over medium heat, stirring constantly.

AMBER SAUCE

1 cup packed brown sugar
1/2 cup light corn syrup
1/2 cup half-and-half
1/4 cup margarine or butter

Mix all ingredients in 1-quart saucepan. Cook over low heat 5 minutes, stirring occasionally. Serve warm.

Nutrition Information Per Serving

1 serving

Calories	450	Fat, g	20
Protein, g	6	Cholesterol, mg	60
Carbohydrate, g	62	Sodium, mg	450

Bread Pudding with Whiskey Sauce

Farm-style Oatmeal Cookies

2 cups packed brown sugar

1 cup lard or shortening

½ cup buttermilk

1 teaspoon vanilla

4 cups quick-cooking oats

1¾ cups all-purpose or whole wheat flour

1 teaspoon baking soda

¾ teaspoon salt

Heat oven to 375°. Mix brown sugar, lard, buttermilk and vanilla in 3-quart bowl. Stir in remaining ingredients. Shape dough into 1-inch balls. Place about 3 inches apart on ungreased cookie sheet. Flatten cookies with bottom of glass dipped in water. Bake until golden brown, 8 to 10 minutes. Immediately remove from cookie sheet. *About 7 dozen cookies.*

Nutrition Information Per Serving

1 cookie

Calories	70	Fat, g	3
Protein, g	1	Cholesterol, mg	2
Carbohydrate, g	10	Sodium, mg	30

Joe Froggers

1 cup sugar

½ cup shortening

1 cup dark molasses

½ cup water

4 cups all-purpose flour

1½ teaspoons salt

1½ teaspoons ground ginger

1 teaspoon baking soda

½ teaspoon ground cloves

½ teaspoon ground nutmeg

¼ teaspoon ground allspice

Sugar

Mix 1 cup sugar, the shortening, molasses and water in 3-quart bowl. Stir in remaining ingredients except sugar. Cover and refrigerate at least 2 hours.

Heat oven to 375°. Roll dough ¼ inch thick on well-floured cloth-covered board. Cut into 3-inch circles; sprinkle with sugar. Place about 1½ inches apart on ungreased cookie sheet. Bake until almost no indentation remains when touched, 10 to 12 minutes. Cool 2 minutes; remove from cookie sheet. Cool completely. *About 3 dozen cookies.*

Nutrition Information Per Serving

1 cookie

Calories	130	Fat, g	3
Protein, g	1	Cholesterol, mg	0
Carbohydrate, g	25	Sodium, mg	115

Joe Froggers

Snickerdoodles

1¹/₂ cups sugar

*¹/₂ cup (1 stick) margarine or butter,
    softened*

¹/₂ cup shortening

2 eggs

2³/₄ cups all-purpose flour

2 teaspoons cream of tartar

1 teaspoon baking soda

¹/₄ teaspoon salt

2 tablespoons sugar

2 teaspoons ground cinnamon

Heat oven to 400°. Mix 1¹/₂ cups sugar, the margarine, shortening and eggs thoroughly in 3-quart bowl. Stir in flour, cream of tartar, baking soda and salt until blended. Shape dough by rounded teaspoonfuls into balls.

Mix 2 tablespoon sugar and the cinnamon; roll balls in sugar mixture. Place about 2 inches apart on ungreased cookie sheet. Bake until set, 8 to 10 minutes. Immediately remove from cookie sheet. *About 6 dozen cookies.*

Nutrition Information Per Serving

1 cookie

Calories	65	Fat, g	3
Protein, g	1	Cholesterol, mg	5
Carbohydrate, g	8	Sodium, mg	40

Deluxe Brownies

The origin of the brownie is shrouded in mystery—was the first batch of brownies really a fallen chocolate cake? In any event, brownies made their appearance sometime after World War I and have been fantastically popular ever since. Whether you're baking up a batch to welcome your new neighbors, to bring to a bake sale or party, or for dessert at home, you know that the rich, chewy, deep chocolate squares will always be real crowd pleasers. Eat them plain or dress them up with a drizzle of chocolate syrup, a scoop of your favorite ice cream or a dollop of luxurious whipped cream and a cherry.

²/₃ cup margarine or butter

*5 ounces unsweetened chocolate, cut
    into pieces*

1³/₄ cups sugar

2 teaspoons vanilla

3 eggs

1 cup all-purpose flour

1 cup chopped nuts

Heat oven to 350°. Grease square pan, 9 × 9 × 2 inches. Heat margarine and chocolate over low heat, stirring constantly, until melted; cool slightly. Beat sugar, vanilla and eggs on high speed 5 minutes. Beat in chocolate mixture on low speed. Beat in flour just until blended. Stir in nuts. Spread in pan. Bake just until brownies begin to pull away from sides of pan, 40 to 45 minutes; cool. Cut into 2-inch squares. *16 brownies.*

Nutrition Information Per Serving

1 brownie

Calories	300	Fat, g	18
Protein, g	3	Cholesterol, mg	40
Carbohydrate, g	31	Sodium, mg	100

Peanut Brittle

Peanut Brittle brings to mind country fairs, freshly squeezed lemonade and making candy with Grandma. Peanut Brittle, so-called because of its texture, was originally a southern specialty, but now enjoys nation-wide popularity. Peanuts, the key ingredient, grow in pods that are formed when the flowers of the peanut plant bury themselves underground. Actually a kind of legume, not a real nut, peanuts were grown by the Cherokees in sections of Georgia, Tennessee and North Carolina.

1¹/₂ teaspoons baking soda

1 teaspoon water

1 teaspoon vanilla

1¹/₂ cups sugar

1 cup water

1 cup light corn syrup

3 tablespoons margarine or butter

1 pound shelled unroasted peanuts

Butter 2 cookie sheets, 15¹/₂ × 12 inches; keep warm in 200° oven. Mixing baking soda, 1 teaspoon water and the vanilla; reserve. Mix sugar, 1 cup water and the corn syrup in 3-quart saucepan. Cook over medium heat, stirring occasionally, to 240° on candy thermometer (or until small amount of mixture dropped into very cold water forms a soft ball that flattens when removed from water).

Stir in margarine and peanuts. Cook, stirring constantly, to 300° (or until small amount of mixture dropped into very cold water separates into threads that are hard and brittle). Watch carefully so mixture does not burn. Immediately remove from heat; stir in baking soda mixture.

Pour half of the candy mixture onto each cookie sheet and quickly spread about ¹/₄ inch thick; cool. Break into pieces. *About 6 dozen candies.*

Nutrition Information Per Serving

1 candy

Calories	80	Fat, g	4
Protein, g	2	Cholesterol, mg	0
Carbohydrate, g	9	Sodium, mg	25

Pralines

2 cups packed light brown sugar

1 cup granulated sugar

1¹/₄ cups milk

¹/₄ cup light corn syrup

¹/₈ teaspoon salt

1 teaspoon vanilla

1¹/₂ cups pecan halves (about 5¹/₂ ounces)

Heat sugars, milk, corn syrup and salt to boiling in 3-quart saucepan, stirring constantly. Cook, without stirring, to 236° on candy thermometer (or until small amount of mixture dropped into very cold water forms a soft ball that flattens when removed from water). Immediately remove thermometer. Cool, without stirring, until saucepan is cool to touch, about 1¹/₂ hours.

Add vanilla and pecans. Beat with spoon until mixture is slightly thickened and just coats pecans but does not lose its gloss, about 1 minute. Drop by spoonfuls onto waxed paper. (Try to divide pecans equally.) Cool until candies are firm and no longer glossy, 12 to 18 hours. Wrap individually in plastic wrap or waxed paper and store tightly covered at room temperature. *About 1¹/₂ dozen candies.*

Nutrition Information Per Serving

1 candy

Calories	220	Fat, g	6
Protein, g	1	Cholesterol, mg	2
Carbohydrate, g	40	Sodium, mg	35

METRIC CONVERSION GUIDE

U.S. UNITS	CANADIAN METRIC	AUSTRALIAN METRIC
Volume		
1/4 teaspoon	1 mL	1 ml
1/2 teaspoon	2 mL	2 ml
1 teaspoon	5 mL	5 ml
1 tablespoon	15 mL	20 ml
1/4 cup	50 mL	60 ml
1/3 cup	75 mL	80 ml
1/2 cup	125 mL	125 ml
2/3 cup	150 mL	170 ml
3/4 cup	175 mL	190 ml
1 cup	250 mL	250 ml
1 quart	1 liter	1 liter
1 1/2 quarts	1.5 liter	1.5 liter
2 quarts	2 liters	2 liters
2 1/2 quarts	2.5 liters	2.5 liters
3 quarts	3 liters	3 liters
4 quarts	4 liters	4 liters
Weight		
1 ounce	30 grams	30 grams
2 ounces	55 grams	60 grams
3 ounces	85 grams	90 grams
4 ounces (1/4 pound)	115 grams	125 grams
8 ounces (1/2 pound)	225 grams	225 grams
16 ounces (1 pound)	455 grams	500 grams
1 pound	455 grams	1/2 kilogram

Measurements

Inches	Centimeters
1	2.5
2	5.0
3	7.5
4	10.0
5	12.5
6	15.0
7	17.5
8	20.5
9	23.0
10	25.5
11	28.0
12	30.5
13	33.0
14	35.5
15	38.0

Temperatures

Fahrenheit	Celsius
32°	0°
212°	100°
250°	120°
275°	140°
300°	150°
325°	160°
350°	180°
375°	190°
400°	200°
425°	220°
450°	230°
475°	240°
500°	260°

NOTE

The recipes in this cookbook have not been developed or tested using metric measures. When converting recipes to metric, some variations in quality may be noted.

Index

Page numbers in *italics* indicate photographs.